ELON
MUSK
AND THE QUEST FOR A
FANTASTIC FUTURE

YOUNG READERS' EDITION

ELON MUSK

AND THE QUEST FOR A FANTASTIC FUTURE

YOUNG READERS' EDITION

ASHLEE VANCE

HARPER

An Imprint of HarperCollinsPublishers

Library of Congress Control Number: 2016949898
ISBN 978-0-06-286243-3

Typography by Chelsea C. Donaldson
18 19 20 21 22   CG/BRR   10 9 8 7 6 5 4 3 2 1

Revised paperback edition, 2018

FOR BOWIE AND TUCKER

1

DINNER WITH ELON

"DO YOU THINK I'M INSANE?"

This question came from Elon Musk near the end of a dinner we shared at a fancy seafood restaurant in Palo Alto, California. I'd gotten to the restaurant first and settled down, knowing Musk would—as always—be late. After about fifteen minutes, Musk showed up wearing designer jeans, a plaid dress shirt, and leather shoes.

Musk stands six foot one, but ask anyone who knows him and they'll tell you he seems much bigger than that. He's extremely broad-shouldered, sturdy, and thick. You might guess that he would strut when entering a room. Instead, he tends to be almost sheepish. This time, he walked with his head tilted down, gave me a quick handshake hello, and then sat at the table. From there, Musk needed a few minutes before he warmed up and looked at ease.

Musk asked me to dinner to negotiate. Eighteen months earlier, I'd informed him of my plans to write a book about him. He'd informed me of his plans not to cooperate and do interviews for the book. His rejection stung at the time but made me work harder as a reporter. I'd spent the last year and a half digging for sources of information and poring over Musk's life. Plenty of people had left Musk's companies—PayPal, Tesla Motors, and SpaceX—and agreed to talk to me. Plus, I already knew a lot of his friends, and they too had plenty of stories to share.

It was after interviewing about two hundred of these people that I heard from Musk again. He called me at home one evening and said that things could go one of two ways: he could start blocking people from talking to me or he could help with the project after all. I, of course, said I preferred the second option.

Musk said he'd be willing to cooperate if he could read the book before it went to publication and could add footnotes throughout it. He would not change my text, but he wanted the chance to set the record straight in spots that he judged inaccurate.

I understood where this was coming from. Musk

wanted control over his life story. He's also a physicist by training and hates factual errors. Any mistake in the book would gnaw away at him for months or even years. While I could understand his perspective, I could not let him read the book. A journalist must have the freedom to research a subject and then present the findings to the world without the fear of someone looking over his shoulder and possibly trying to tilt the work in his favor. Besides that, Musk has his version of the truth, and it often differs from the view held by others. Lastly, Musk tends to give very long answers to even basic questions, and the thought of footnotes that were longer than the actual book seemed all too real.

The fancy dinner was our chance to chat all of this out, have a bit of a debate, and see where it left us.

When the dinner first started, we talked for a while about people we both knew, famous businessmen like Howard Hughes, and the Tesla car factory. About twenty minutes in, the waiter stopped by to take our order, and Musk asked for suggestions that would work with his diet. At the time, he did the whole low-carb thing and tried to avoid foods like pasta, bread, and sugary treats. He settled on chunks of fried lobster coated with black squid ink.

Even before our negotiation had really begun, Musk started talking and opening up in his uniquely serious fashion. He confessed to being terrified that Google's cofounder Larry Page might be building a fleet of artificial-intelligence-enhanced robots capable of destroying mankind. "I'm really worried about this," Musk said.

It didn't make Musk feel any better that he and Page were very close friends and that he felt Page was a good person. In fact, that was sort of the problem. Page's nice-guy nature left him assuming that the machines would forever do what we wanted. "I'm not as optimistic," Musk said. "He could produce something evil by accident."

When the food arrived, Musk consumed it. That is, he didn't eat it as much as he made it disappear rapidly with a few huge bites. Wanting to keep Musk happy and chatting, I handed him a big chunk of steak from my plate. The plan worked . . . for all of ninety seconds. Meat. Hunk. Gone.

It took a while to redirect Musk's thoughts on robots taking over humanity, and get him to talk about the book. Once he did, Musk immediately asked why it was that I wanted to write about him. I had been waiting for this moment. Excited, I launched into what was meant to be a forty-five-minute speech about all the reasons Musk should let me invade his life. And that he should allow this intrusion while getting none of the controls he wanted in return. To my great surprise, Musk cut me off after a couple of minutes and simply said, "Okay."

The dinner ended with pleasant conversation and

Musk abandoning his healthy diet for a giant cotton candy dessert sculpture. It was settled. Musk would allow me to talk to the executives at his companies, his friends, and his family. He would meet me for dinner once a month for as long as it took to complete the book project. For the first time, Musk would let a reporter see the inner workings of his world.

Two and a half hours after we started, Musk put his hands on the table, made a move to get up, and then paused. He locked eyes with me and asked that incredible question: "Do you think I'm insane?" The strangeness of the question left me speechless for a moment while I tried to figure out if this was some sort of riddle. It was only after I'd later spent lots of time with Musk that I realized the question was more for him than me. Nothing I said would have mattered. Musk was stopping one last time and wondering aloud if I could be trusted and then looking into my eyes to make his judgment. A split second later, we shook hands and Musk drove off in a red Tesla Model S sedan.

2

ELON'S WORLD

ANY STUDY OF ELON MUSK must begin at the headquarters of his rocket company, SpaceX, in Hawthorne, California—a suburb of Los Angeles. It's there that visitors will find two giant posters of Mars hanging side by side on the wall near Musk's office. The poster to the left depicts Mars as it is today—a cold, empty red orb. The poster on the right shows an imagined version of Mars with a giant green landmass surrounded by oceans. The planet has been heated up and made habitable for humans.

Musk wants this to happen. Turning humans into space colonizers is his stated life's purpose. He wants a backup plan for the human species in case something goes terribly wrong on Earth—be it an unforeseen disaster like an asteroid crashing into the planet or a terrible disease that wipes out billions of people or an issue such as global warming that's caused by humans. "I would like to die thinking that humanity has a bright future," he said. "If we can solve sustainable energy and be well on our way to becoming a multiplanetary species with a self-sustaining civilization on another planet—to cope with a worst-case scenario happening and extinguishing human conscious-ness—then," and here he paused for a moment, "I think that would be really good."

If some of the things that Musk says and does sound absurd, it's because on one level they very much are. Musk's willingness to tackle extraordinarily difficult things has turned him into an idol in Silicon Valley, the center of technological advancement in the United States. There, fel-low businessmen like Larry Page speak of him in glowing terms, and young entrepreneurs strive "to be like Elon."

Outside of Silicon Valley, people often view Musk with more doubt. They tend to think of Musk as the guy who has gotten rich from not very useful or practical electric cars, solar panels, and rockets.

Yet, in the early part of 2012, even the doubters began to realize what Musk was actually accomplishing. His companies were succeeding at things that had never been done before. SpaceX flew a supply capsule to the

International Space Station (ISS) and brought it safely back to Earth. His car company, Tesla Motors, delivered the Model S, a beautiful, all-electric sedan that amazed the automotive industry. Musk was also the chairman and largest shareholder (or owner of the company's stock) of SolarCity, a growing solar energy company. Musk had somehow delivered the biggest advances the space, automotive, and energy industries had seen in decades in what felt like one fell swoop.

It's difficult to believe that Hawthorne, California, could serve as the home base for all of this drive, ambition, and high energy. It's an ugly part of Los Angeles County in which run-down buildings surround more run-down buildings. But, sure enough, in the middle of these grim surroundings stands a gleaming, 550,000-square-foot white rectangle. This is the main SpaceX building.

During my first visit to SpaceX, I found hundreds of engineers and mechanics making multiple rockets at a time—from scratch. The factory was a massive, open work area. Near the back were huge delivery bays that allowed for the arrival of hunks of metal, which were transported to two-story-high welding machines. Over to one side were technicians in white coats making motherboards, radios, and more electronics.

Other people were in a special, airtight glass chamber,

building the capsules that rockets would take to the International Space Station. Tattooed men in bandannas were blasting rock music and threading wires around rocket engines. There were completed bodies of rockets lined up one after the other, ready to be placed on trucks. Still more rockets, in another part of the building, awaited coats of white paint. It was difficult to take in the entire factory at once. There were bodies in constant motion whirring around a variety of bizarre machines.

Musk's companies operate out of several other buildings nearby as well. One of these buildings has a curved roof and looks like an airplane hangar. It serves as the research, development, and design studio for Tesla. This is where the company came up with the look for the Model S sedan and its follow-on, the Model X SUV. In the parking lot outside the studio, Tesla has built one of its charging stations, where Los Angeles drivers can top up with electricity for free.

It was in my first interview with Musk, which took place at the design studio, that I began to get a sense of how he talked and operated. He's a confident guy, but can come off as shy and awkward. He has a slight South African accent and, like many engineers, will pause while thinking of the exact word he wants. He also has a tendency to speak about technical things in technical terms with no simplified explanations along the way. Musk expects you to keep up.

None of this is off-putting. Musk, in fact, will tell plenty of jokes and can be very charming. It's just that there's a sense of purpose and pressure hanging over any conversation with the man. Musk doesn't really do small talk.

Most famous businessmen have assistants surrounding them. Musk mostly moves about SpaceX and Tesla on his own. Inside his companies, he's nothing like the Musk who slinks across a restaurant. He's the guy who owns the joint and strides about with authority.

Musk and I talked as he made his way around the design studio's main floor, inspecting parts and vehicles. At each station, employees rushed up to Musk and spewed information at him. He listened intently, processed it, and nodded when satisfied. The people moved away, and Musk shifted over to the next information dump.

At one point, Tesla's design chief, Franz von Holzhausen, wanted Musk's take on the seating arrangements for the Model X. As they spoke, a couple of workers jotted down notes, and then they went into a back room and listened to executives from a seller of high-end graphics software trying to convince Musk to buy their products.

After that, Musk walked toward the source of a ton of loud noise—a workshop deep in the design studio where Tesla engineers were building part of the thirty-foot decorative towers that go outside the charging stations. "That thing looks like it could survive a Category Five hurricane," Musk said. "Let's thin it up a bit." Musk and I eventually hopped into his car—a black Model S—and zipped back to the main SpaceX building. He described some more worries about the state of the technology industry, and said he'd like to see more people build machines and breakthrough devices. "I think there are probably too many smart people pursuing internet stuff, finance, and law," Musk said on the way. "That is part of the reason why we haven't seen as much innovation."

Musk Land was a revelation. It was the very thing I'd been searching for since coming to San Francisco as a reporter fifteen years earlier.

San Francisco has a long history with greed. It became a city on the back of the gold rush, with thousands upon thousands of people arriving to try and make their fortunes. Economic highs and lows are the rhythm of this place. And in 2000, San Francisco had been overtaken by the highest of all economic highs, the dot-com boom. The entire populace gave in to a fantasy—a get-rich-quick internet madness. You could feel the energy from this shared delusion. It produced a constant buzz that vibrated across the city.

You no longer had to make something that other people wanted to buy in order to start a solid company. You just had to have an idea for some sort of internet thing in order for investors to fund you. The whole goal was to make as much money as possible in the shortest amount of time because everyone knew that reality had to set in eventually, and the good times would end.

The collapse of the get-rich-quick internet fantasy in 2001 left San Francisco and Silicon Valley in a deep depression. The technology industry had no idea what to do with itself. The investors who had lost huge amounts of money didn't want to look any dumber and make more mistakes, so they stopped funding new ventures altogether. Businesspeople stopped trying to woo investors with daring product proposals, and instead pitched small, flimsy things that they thought might be more attractive in these conservative times.

The evidence of this slump in innovation can be seen in the companies and ideas formed during this period. Google had appeared and really started to thrive around 2002, but it was unique. Between Google, and then Apple's introduction of the iPhone in 2007, there's a wasteland of ho-hum companies. And the hot new things that were just starting out—Facebook and Twitter—certainly did not look like the companies that had come before—Hewlett-Packard, Intel, Sun Microsystems. Those companies made physical products and employed tens of thousands of people in the process. The goal of the new generation of companies had shifted from taking huge risks and creating new industries to pumping out simple apps and trying to entertain consumers while making money from advertisements on a website. "The best minds of my generation are thinking about how to make people click ads," Jeff Hammerbacher, an early Facebook engineer, told me. "That sucks."

By rights, Musk should have been part of the slump and this way of thinking. He jumped right into the internet frenzy in 1995. Then, fresh out of college, he started a company called Zip2—an early, less advanced version of Yelp. That first company ended up a big, quick hit. Musk made $22 million from Zip2's sale and poured almost all of it into his next company, a start-up that would eventually become PayPal, the popular online finance service. As the largest shareholder in PayPal, Musk became fantastically rich when eBay acquired the company for $1.5 billion in 2002.

Instead of hanging around Silicon Valley and falling into the same funk as his peers, however, Musk moved to Los Angeles. He threw $100 million into SpaceX, $70 million into Tesla, and $10 million into SolarCity. Short of building an actual money-crushing machine, Musk could not have picked a faster way to destroy his fortune. All of these companies were thought to be too risky and too hard. Moreover, he was making supercomplex physical goods in two of the most expensive places in the world, Los Angeles and Silicon Valley. This came at a time when many people said the United States could no longer compete against countries like China when it came to manufacturing things.

Musk, though, pushed ahead and turned manufacturing into a major edge for his companies. SpaceX and Tesla build as much as possible at their own facilities rather than turning to partners. Musk's companies ended up rethinking many of the methods that the traditional aerospace, automotive, and solar industries had accepted as the way things are done.

With SpaceX, Musk is sending satellites and supplies into space aboard towering rockets. He's competing with the giants that serve the US military, including aerospace companies like Lockheed Martin and Boeing. He's also competing against entire nations—most notably Russia and China. SpaceX has made a name for itself as the cheapest rocket launch provider in the industry. But that, in and of itself, is not really good enough to win. The space business comes with a complex set of politics too, in which companies must win over legislators in Washington, DC, and so Musk has needed to learn skills of persuasion as well.

SpaceX has been testing reusable rockets that can

carry loads to space and land back on Earth, on their launchpads, with precision. If the company can perfect this technology, it will deal a devastating blow to all of its competitors while making the United States the world leader for taking cargo and humans to space. It's a threat that Musk figures has earned him plenty of fierce enemies. "The list of people that would not mind if I was gone is growing," Musk said. "My family fears that the Russians will assassinate me."

With Tesla Motors, Musk has tried to revolutionize the way cars are manufactured and sold. Musk refused to focus on hybrids that run on both gas and electricity, which he views as an imperfect compromise. Instead, Tesla makes all-electric cars that people long for and that push the limits of technology.

With SolarCity, Musk has funded the largest installer of solar panels for houses and businesses. Musk helped come up with the idea for SolarCity and serves as its chairman. During a time in which clean-tech businesses have failed with frightening regularity, Musk has built two of the most successful clean-tech companies in the world. (Musk, in fact, merged Tesla and SolarCity into one company in 2016.)

Musk's empire of factories, tens of thousands of workers, and industrial strength have shaken up three different industries. They have also turned Musk into one of the richest men ever, with a net worth of more than $10 billion.

My first visit to SpaceX started to make a few things clear about how Musk had pulled all this off. While Musk's goal to put men on Mars can seem strange, it's a lofty ambition that really helps to motivate his employees. In fact, the workers at all three of Musk's companies are aware that they're trying to achieve monumental things day in and day out, and it keeps them going. When Musk sets unrealistic goals or works employees to the bone, it's because he is trying to . . . well . . . save the human race.

The life that Musk has created to manage all of these endeavors is ridiculous. A typical week starts at his mansion in Bel Air, an exclusive enclave of Los Angeles. On Monday, he works the entire day at SpaceX. On Tuesday, he begins at SpaceX, then hops onto his jet and flies to Silicon Valley in Northern California. He spends a couple of days working at Tesla, which has its offices in Palo Alto and factory in Fremont. Musk does not own a home in Silicon Valley and ends up staying at a hotel or at friends' houses. To arrange the stays with friends, Musk's assistant will send an email asking, "Room for one?" and if the friend says, "Yes," Musk turns up at the door late at night. Most often he stays in a guest room, but he's also been known to crash on the couch after winding down with some video games. Then it's back to Los Angeles and SpaceX on Thursday.

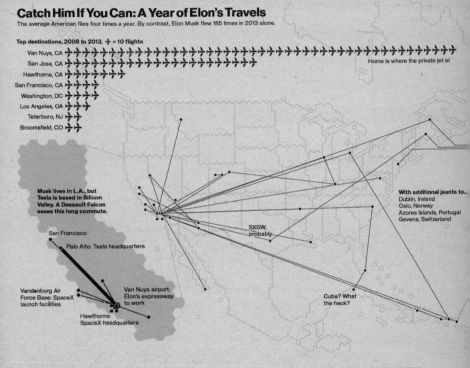

Catch Him If You Can: A Year of Elon's Travels

The average American flies four times a year. By contrast, Elon Musk flew 185 times in 2013 alone.

Top destinations, 2008 to 2013. ✈ = 10 flights

Van Nuys, CA ✈✈
San Jose, CA ✈✈✈✈✈✈✈✈✈✈✈✈✈✈✈✈✈✈✈✈✈✈✈✈✈
Hawthorne, CA ✈✈✈✈✈✈
San Francisco, CA ✈✈✈✈✈
Washington, DC ✈✈✈✈
Los Angeles, CA ✈✈✈
Teterboro, NJ ✈✈
Broomsfield, CO ✈✈

Home is where the private jet is!

Musk lives in L.A., but Tesla is based in Silicon Valley. A Dassault Falcon eases this long commute.

San Francisco
Palo Alto: Tesla headquarters
Vandenburg Air Force Base: SpaceX launch facilities
Van Nuys airport: Elon's expressway to work
Hawthorne: SpaceX headquarters

SXSW, probably
Cuba? What the heck?

With additional jaunts to..
Dublin, Ireland
Oslo, Norway
Azores Islands, Portugal
Gevena, Switzerland

Musk is a nonstop traveler. Here's a look at one year in his life via records obtained through a Freedom of Information Act request.

When asked how he survives this schedule, Musk said, "I had a tough childhood, so maybe that was helpful."

Musk has taken industries like aerospace and automotive that America seemed to have given up on and changed them into something new and fantastic. At the heart of this transformation are Musk's skills as a software maker and his ability to apply them to machines.

He's merged atoms—physical stuff—and bits—code—in ways that few people thought possible, and the results have been spectacular.

"To me, Elon is the shining example of how Silicon Valley might be able to reinvent itself," said Edward Jung, a famed software engineer and inventor. "We need to look at different models of how to do things that are longer term in nature and where the technology is more integrated." The integration mentioned by Jung—the melding of software, electronics, advanced materials, and computing horsepower—appears to be Musk's gift.

And Musk is using his gift to make astonishing machines. Because of Musk, Americans could wake up in ten years with the most modern highway in the world: a system run by thousands of solar-powered charging stations and traveled by electric cars. By that time, SpaceX may well be sending up rockets every day, taking people and things to dozens of space habitats, and making preparations for longer treks to Mars. These advances are difficult to imagine, but seem to some degree inevitable with Musk in the picture. As his first wife, Justine, put it, "He does what he wants, and he is relentless about it. It's Elon's world, and the rest of us live in it."

3

ADVENTURES IN AFRICA

THE PUBLIC FIRST MET ELON Reeve Musk in 1984. A South African magazine published the code to a video game a twelve-year-old Musk had designed. Called Blastar, the science-fiction-inspired space game required 167 lines of instructions to run. This was back in the day when early computer users were required to type out commands to make their machines do much of anything. In that context, Musk's game did not shine as a marvel of computer science, but it was certainly better than what most youngsters at the time could manage.

Musk's original video game he wrote as a twelve year old and published in a local magazine.
© Maye Musk

The Blastar game illustrates how Musk already had visions of grand conquests dancing in his head. A brief explanation written by Musk stated, "In this game you have to destroy an alien space freighter, which is carrying deadly Hydrogen Bombs and Status Beam Machines. This game makes good use of sprites and animation, and in this sense makes the listing worth reading." (As of this writing, not even the internet knows what "status beam machines" are.)

A boy fantasizing about space and battles between good and evil isn't anything new. A boy who takes these thoughts seriously is more remarkable. Such was the case with the young Elon Musk. By the middle of his teenage years, Musk had come to see guarding man's fate in the universe as a personal obligation. If that meant he must improve clean energy to keep man alive on Earth or build spaceships to extend the human species' reach, then so be it. Musk would find a way to make these things happen.

"Maybe I read too many comics as a kid," Musk said. "In the comics, it always seems like they are trying to save the world. It seemed like one should try to make the world a better place because the inverse makes no sense."

At around age fourteen, Musk became influenced by the sci-fi lessons in the book *The Hitchhiker's Guide to the Galaxy* by Douglas Adams. "[The book] points out that one of the really tough things is figuring out what questions to ask," Musk said. "Once you figure out the question, then the answer is relatively easy. I came to the conclusion that really we should aspire to increase the scope and scale of human consciousness in order to better understand what questions to ask." The teenage Musk then arrived at the stated meaning for his life. "The only thing that makes sense to do is strive for greater collective enlightenment," he said.

Born in 1971, Musk grew up in Pretoria, a large city in South Africa. At the time, South Africa operated under the specter of apartheid—a racist government-backed policy that called for the separation of whites and nonwhites. The brutal, unfair nature of apartheid resulted in a country full of tension, and this often boiled over into protests and other violent clashes.

These heated times influenced some of Musk's thinking, and so too did the white Afrikaner culture that was dominant in Pretoria. Extremely masculine behavior was celebrated, and tough jocks were considered cool. Young men spent much of their time on the rugby field and the cricket pitch.

Even though his family was well-off financially and Musk did not want for things, Musk did not fit in to this world. He never took to sports or sought out the attention of his male peers. He preferred to creep off toward a corner somewhere and settle down with a book—often a science-fiction one. Other kids made fun of him for his shy personality and geeky interests.

Musk, almost from his earliest days, planned to escape

South Africa. He longed for a place where he could be himself and make his dreams come true. Even then he had visions of traveling to space or running an ambitious company. He, like many, saw America as the land of opportunity and the most likely spot to put his plans in motion. Specifically, Musk heard a lot about Silicon Valley—this place in California where people did wonderful things with technology. He decided that he would one day call Silicon Valley home. This is how a lonely, awkward South African boy—who talked about pursuing "collective enlightenment"—ended up as America's most adventurous industrialist.

Adventure and risk-taking seem to have been programmed into Musk's genes. His mom's father, Joshua Haldeman, was born in Canada and was known to ride broncos, box, and wrestle. As a youngster, Joshua would break in horses for local farmers and help out with other demanding tasks on the prairies. He also organized one of Canada's first rodeos and tried his hand at politics before settling down as a chiropractor.

Elon's grandfather Joshua married a Canadian dance instructor, Winnifred Fletcher, or Wyn. In 1948, the family, which already included a son and a daughter, welcomed twin daughters Kaye and Maye, Musk's mother. Ever in search of something new to do, Joshua picked up flying and bought his own plane. The family gained some measure of notoriety as people heard about Joshua and his wife packing their kids into the back of the single-engine airplane and heading off on excursions all around North America.

Joshua seemed to have everything going for him when, in 1950, he decided to give it all away. The former politician had come to disagree with many of Canada's policies, seeing the government as too meddlesome in the lives of its citizens. To go along with these gripes, Joshua also possessed an enduring lust for adventure that convinced him the time was right to leave Canada.

Over the course of a few months, the family sold their house and possessions and decided to move to South Africa—a place Joshua had never been. Joshua disassembled the family's airplane and put it into crates to ship it to Africa. Once there, the family rebuilt the plane and used it to scour the country for a nice place to live, ultimately settling in Pretoria.

The family's spirit for adventure seemed to know no bounds. In 1952, Joshua and Wyn made a twenty-two-thousand-mile round-trip journey in their plane, flying up through Africa to Scotland and Norway. Wyn served as the navigator and would sometimes take over the flying duties. The couple topped this effort in 1954, flying thirty thousand miles to Australia and back. Newspapers reported on the couple's trip, and they're believed to be the only private pilots to get from Africa to Australia in a single-engine plane.

The Haldeman children had lots of downtime in the African bush while on wild adventures with their parents. © Maye Musk

When not up in the air, the Haldemans were out in the African wilderness. They would go on great, monthlong expeditions to find the Lost City of the Kalahari Desert, a supposed abandoned city in southern Africa. During one trip, the family's truck hit a tree stump, pushing the bumper backward into the radiator. Stuck in the middle of nowhere with no means of communication, Joshua worked for three days to fix the truck while the rest of the family hunted for food. On other trips, hyenas and leopards would circle the campfire at night. One morning, the family woke to find a lion three feet away from their main table. Joshua grabbed the first object he could find—a lamp—waved it, and told the lion to go away. And it did.

Joshua died in 1974 at the age of seventy-two. He'd been doing practice landings in his plane and didn't see a wire running between a pair of poles. The wire caught the plane's wheels and flipped the craft. Joshua broke his neck.

Elon was a toddler at the time of the death and has only a slight recollection of Joshua. But throughout his childhood, Elon heard many stories about his grandfather's adventures and reveled in the excitement of the family's wild life. "My grandmother told these tales of how they almost died several times along their journeys," Musk said. "They were flying in a plane with literally no instruments—not even a radio—and they had road maps instead of aerial maps, and some of those weren't even correct. My grandfather had this desire for adventure, exploration, doing crazy things." Elon buys into the idea that his unusual tolerance for risk may well have been inherited directly from his grandfather.

Maye Musk, Elon's mother, adored her parents and shared their zest for life. In her youth, she was considered a nerd. She liked math and science and did well in her course work. By the age of fifteen, however, people noticed something else about her. Tall with ash-blond hair, Maye had high cheekbones and angular features that would make her stand out anywhere. On the weekends, Maye modeled in runway shows and magazine shoots. She ended up as a finalist for Miss South Africa.

Maye and Errol Musk, Elon's father, grew up in the same neighborhood, and knew each other throughout their youth. Years later, they married and then Maye gave birth to Elon on June 28, 1971. Errol worked as an engineer—and a very good one at that. He developed large projects such as office buildings and retail complexes. Maye set up a practice as a dietitian. A bit more than a year after Elon's birth came his brother, Kimbal, and soon thereafter came their sister, Tosca.

Elon showed all the traits of a curious, energetic tot. He picked things up easily, and Maye, like many mothers do, considered her son brilliant. "He seemed to understand things quicker than the other kids," she said. The weird thing was that Elon appeared to drift off into a trance at times. People spoke to him, but nothing got through when he had a certain distant look in his eyes. This happened so often that Elon's parents and doctors thought he might be deaf. "Sometimes, he just didn't hear you," said Maye. Doctors ran a series of tests on Elon. They finally elected to remove the adenoid glands in the roof of his mouth, which can improve hearing in children. "Well, it didn't change," said Maye.

As a toddler, Musk would often drift into his own world and ignore those around him. Doctors thought he might be hard of hearing and had his adenoid glands removed. © Maye Musk

Elon's condition had far more to do with the wiring of his mind than his ears. "He goes into his brain, and then you just see he is in another world," Maye said. "He still does that. Now I just leave him be because I know he is designing a new rocket or something."

Other children did not understand these dreamlike states. You could do jumping jacks right beside Musk, and he would not even notice. He kept on thinking. Those around him judged that he was either rude or really weird. "I do think Elon was always a little different, but in a nerdy way," Maye said.

28

For Musk, these thoughtful moments were wonderful. At five and six, he had found a way to block out the world and concentrate on only a single task. He could clearly see images in his head in extraordinary detail. "It seems as though the part of the brain that's usually reserved for visual processing—the part that is used to process images coming in from my eyes—gets taken over by internal thought processes," Musk said.

Over time, Musk has ended up thinking that his brain is similar to a computer. It allows him to see things out in the world, copy them in his mind, and imagine how they might be changed or used. The unique way that his brain works helps him grapple with difficult physics concepts and engineering problems. "Acceleration, momentum, kinetic energy—how those sorts of things will be affected by objects comes through very vividly," Musk said.

The most striking thing about Elon as a young boy was his need to read. From a very young age, he seemed to have a book in his hands at all times. "It was not unusual for him to read ten hours a day," said Kimbal. "If it was the weekend, he could go through two books in a day." The family went on numerous shopping excursions in which they realized midtrip that Elon had gone missing. Maye or Kimbal would pop into the nearest bookstore and find Elon.

Somewhere near the back sitting on the floor, he would be reading, oblivious of everything else.

As Elon got older, he would take himself to the bookstore when school ended at two p.m. and stay there until about six p.m. He plowed through fiction books and then comics and then nonfiction titles. "Sometimes they kicked me out of the store, but usually not," Elon said. He listed *The Lord of the Rings* and Robert Heinlein's *The Moon Is a Harsh Mistress* as some of his favorites, along with *The Hitchhiker's Guide to the Galaxy*.

"At one point, I ran out of books to read at the school library and the neighborhood library," Musk said. "This is maybe the third or fourth grade. I tried to convince the librarian to order books for me. So then I started to read the *Encyclopaedia Britannica*. That was so helpful. You don't know what you don't know. You realize there are all these things out there."

Elon, in fact, churned through two sets of encyclopedias—an accomplishment that did little to help him make friends. The boy had a photographic memory, and the encyclopedias turned him into a fact factory. He came off as a classic know-it-all. At the dinner table, his sister would wonder aloud about the distance from Earth to the moon, and Elon would spit out the exact measurement.

"If we had a question, Tosca would always say, 'Just ask genius boy,'" Maye said. "We could ask him about anything. He just remembered it."

As a youngster, Elon's tendency to correct people bothered the other kids. "They would say, 'Elon, we are not playing with you anymore,'" said Maye. "I felt very sad as a mother because I think he wanted friends. Kimbal and Tosca would bring home friends, and Elon wouldn't, and he would want to play with them. But he was awkward, you know."

Maye urged Kimbal and Tosca to include Elon. They responded as kids will. "But, Mom, he's not fun." As he got older, however, Elon would have strong, loving relationships with his siblings and cousins. Though he kept to himself at school, Elon had an outgoing nature with members of his family and eventually became the leader among them.

For a while, life inside the Musk household was quite good. The family owned one of the biggest houses in Pretoria. There's a portrait of the three Musk children taken when Elon was about eight years old that shows three blond, fit children sitting next to one another on a brick porch with Pretoria's famous purple jacaranda trees in the background. Elon has large, rounded cheeks and a broad smile.

Elon, Kimbal, and Tosca at their house in South Africa. © Maye Musk

Then, not long after the photo was taken, his parents separated and divorced in 1980, when Elon was nine. Maye moved with the kids to the family's holiday home in Durban, on South Africa's eastern coast. After a couple of years of this arrangement, Elon decided he wanted to live with his father. "My father seemed sort of sad and lonely, and my mom had three kids, and he didn't have any," Musk said. "It seemed unfair."

The decision baffled his mother. "I could not understand why he would leave this happy home I made for him—this really happy home," said Maye. "But Elon is his own person." Kimbal later decided to live with Errol also, saying simply that sons want to live with their father.

Errol's side of the family has been in South Africa for over two hundred years. Errol's father, Walter Henry James Musk, was an army sergeant. "I remember him almost never talking," Elon said. "He would just . . . be grumpy."

Cora Amelia Musk, Errol's mother, was born in England to a family famous for their intelligence. She adored her grandchildren. "Our grandmother had this very dominant personality," said Kimbal. "She was a very big influence in our lives." Elon considered his relationship with Cora—or Nana, as he called her—particularly tight. "After the divorce, she took care of me quite a lot," he said. "She would pick me up from school, and I would hang out with her playing Scrabble and that type of thing."

On the surface, life at Errol's house seemed grand. Errol had plenty of books for Elon to read and took his children on numerous trips overseas. "I have a lot of fun memories from that," said Kimbal.

Errol also impressed the kids with his intellect and gave them some practical lessons. "He was a talented engineer," Elon said. "He knew how every physical object worked." Both Elon and Kimbal were required to go to the sites of Errol's engineering jobs and learn how to lay bricks, install plumbing, fit windows, and put in electrical wiring. "There were fun moments," Elon said, reflecting on the time spent living with his dad.

Errol could also be tough on his boys. Kimbal described Errol as "ultrapresent and very intense." He would sit Elon and Kimbal down and lecture at them for three to four hours without the boys being able to respond. He seemed to delight in being stern and sucked much of the pleasure out of common childhood diversions.

From time to time, Elon tried to convince his dad to move to America and often talked about his plan to live in the United States later in life. Errol didn't appreciate such talk and tried to convince Elon that life in America would be tough. He sent the family's numerous housekeepers away so that Elon could take on all of the chores and know what it was like "to play American."

Both Elon and Kimbal describe living with their father as difficult. "It was a very emotionally challenging upbringing, but it made us who we are today," Kimbal said.

"It would certainly be accurate to say that I did not have a good childhood," Elon said. "It may sound good. It was not absent of good, but it was not a happy childhood. It was like misery. He's good at making life miserable—that's for sure," Elon said, describing his father. "He can take any situation, no matter how good it is, and make it bad. He's not a happy man. I don't know . . . I don't know how someone becomes like he is."

When upset, Elon would retreat into his books. Then, when he was nearly ten years old, he spotted a computer for the first time and soon had another escape. "There was an electronics store that mostly did hi-fi-type stuff, but then, in one corner, they started stocking a few computers," Musk said. He was amazed by this machine that could be programmed to do whatever a person wanted.

"I had to have that and then hounded my father to get the computer," Musk said. Not long after that chat, he became the proud owner of a Commodore VIC-20, a popular home machine that went on sale in 1980. Elon's computer arrived with five kilobytes of memory and a workbook on the BASIC programming language.

"It was supposed to take like six months to get through all the lessons," Elon said. "I just got super OCD on it and stayed up for three days with no sleep and did the entire thing. It seemed like the most supercompelling thing I had ever seen." Despite being an engineer, Musk's father dismissed the computer as a silly object. "He said it was just for games and that you'd never be able to do real engineering on it," Elon recalled. "I just said, 'Whatever.'"

While bookish and into his new computer, Elon quite often led Kimbal and his cousins (Kaye's children) Russ, Lyndon, and Peter Rive on adventures. They dabbled one year in selling Easter eggs in the neighborhood. The eggs were not well decorated, but the boys still marked them up a few hundred percent for their wealthy neighbors and went door-to-door to find buyers.

Elon also took charge of their experiments with home-made explosives and rockets. Musk would create his own chemical compounds and put them inside of canisters. "It is remarkable how many things you can get to explode," Elon said. "I'm lucky I have all my fingers." When not blowing things up, the boys put on layers of clothing and goggles and shot one another with pellet guns. Elon and Kimbal raced dirt bikes against each other in sandlots until Kimbal flew off his bike one day and hurtled into a barbed wire fence.

As the years went on, Elon and his cousins started to take their business pursuits more seriously. At one point, they even attempted to open a video arcade. Without any parents knowing, the boys picked out a spot for their arcade, got a lease, and started navigating the permit process for their business. Eventually, they had to get someone over eighteen to sign a legal document, and neither the Rives' father nor Errol would sign.

The boys' craziest adventures may have been their trips between Pretoria and Johannesburg. During the 1980s, South Africa could be a terribly violent place, and the thirty-five-mile train trip between Pretoria and Johannes-burg was one of the world's more dangerous rides. "South

Africa was not a happy-go-lucky place," Kimbal said, "and that has an impact on you. We saw some really rough stuff. It was part of an atypical upbringing—just this insane set of experiences that changes how you view risk. You don't grow up thinking getting a job is the hard part. That's not interesting enough."

The boys ranged in age from about thirteen to sixteen. One of their passions was Dungeons & Dragons, a fantasy role-playing game. Once, they went to a Dungeons & Dragons tournament. "That was us being nerd master supremes," Musk said. All of the boys were into Dungeons & Dragons. The game requires someone to help set the mood for a contest by imagining and then describing a scene. "You have entered a room, and there is a chest in the corner. What will you do? . . . You open the chest. You've sprung a trap. Dozens of goblins are on the loose."

Elon excelled at this Dungeon Master role and had memorized the texts describing the powers of monsters and other characters. "Under Elon's leadership, we played the role so well and won the tournament," said Peter Rive. "Winning requires this incredible imagination, and Elon really set the tone for keeping people captivated and inspired."

School was less fun for Elon. He went to a couple different schools during middle and high school and often encountered bullies.

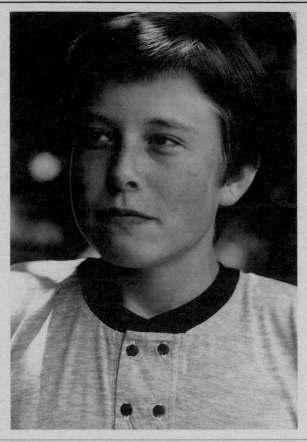

Musk was a loner throughout grade school and suffered for years at the hands of bullies.
© Maye Musk

One afternoon, during eighth grade, Elon and Kimbal were sitting at the top of a flight of concrete stairs, eating, when a boy decided to go after Elon. "I was basically hiding from this gang that was . . . hunting me down . . . I think I accidentally bumped this guy at assembly that morning and he'd taken some huge offense at that," Musk said. The boy crept up behind Musk, kicked him in the head, and then shoved him down the stairs. Musk tumbled down the entire flight, and a handful of boys pounced on him. Some of them kicked Elon in the side, and the ringleader bashed his head against the ground. "They were a bunch of . . . psychos," Musk said. "I blacked out." Kimbal watched in horror and feared for Elon's life. He rushed down the stairs to find Elon's face bloodied and swollen. "He looked like someone who had just been in the boxing ring," Kimbal said. Elon then went to the hospital. "It was about a week before I could get back to school," Musk said.

For three or four years, these bullies hounded Musk. They went so far as to beat up a boy that Musk considered his best friend until the child agreed to stop hanging out with Musk. "Moreover, they got him—they got my best . . . friend—to lure me out of hiding so they could beat me up," Musk said. "And that . . . hurt." While telling this part of the story, Musk's eyes welled up and his voice shook. "For some reason, they decided that I was it, and they were going to go after me nonstop. That's what made growing up difficult. For a number of years, there was no respite. You get chased around by gangs at school who tried to beat . . . me, and then I'd come home, and it would just be awful there as well. It was just like nonstop horrible."

Musk spent the latter parts of his high school at Pretoria Boys High School. Life was more bearable there because Musk had had a growth spurt and the students were generally better behaved. While a public school by definition, Pretoria Boys has functioned more like a private school for the last hundred years. It's the place you send a young man to get him ready to attend Oxford or Cambridge.

The boys from Musk's class remember him as a likable, quiet, unexceptional student. "There were four or five boys that were considered the very brightest," said a boy who sat behind Elon in some classes. "Elon was not one of them." Such comments were echoed by a half dozen kids who also noted that Musk's lack of interest in sports left him alone a lot. "Honestly, there were just no signs that he was going to be a billionaire," said another classmate. "He was never in a leadership position at school. I was rather surprised to see what has happened to him."

While Musk didn't have any close friends at school, his unusual interests did leave an impression. One boy remembered Musk bringing model rockets to school and blasting them off during breaks. During a science class debate, Elon gained attention for arguing against fossil fuels in favor of solar power—a very unpopular argument in South Africa at the time, since the country's economy depends on its rich natural resources. "He always had firm views on things," said a classmate. Terence Beney, a classmate who stayed in touch with Elon over the years, claimed that Musk had started dreaming about sending humans to other planets in high school as well and would talk about these aspirations with his peers.

While Musk might not have been among the best students in his class, he was among a handful of students with the grades and interest to be selected for an experimental computer program. Students were taken out of a number of schools and brought together to learn the BASIC, COBOL, and Pascal programming languages. Musk exceled at the class.

At the same time, Musk continued to love science fiction and fantasy. He tried his hand at writing stories that involved dragons and supernatural beings. "I wanted to write something like *The Lord of the Rings*," he said.

To Maye, Musk did great at school. She can recount plenty of tales where teenage Elon performed fantastic academic feats. According to her, the only reason he did not outrank the other boys on his grades was a lack of interest in the work the school assigned.

Musk largely agrees with his mother's take. He said, "I just looked at it as 'What grades do I need to get where I want to go?' There were compulsory subjects, like Afrikaans, and I just didn't see the point of learning that. It seemed ridiculous. I'd get a passing grade, and that was fine. Things like physics and computers—I got the highest grade you can get in those. There needs to be a reason for a grade. I'd rather play video games, write software, and read books than try and get an A if there's no point in getting an A. I can remember failing subjects in like fourth and fifth grade. Then my mother's boyfriend told me I'd be held back if I didn't pass. I didn't actually know you had to pass the subjects to move to the next grade. I got the best grades in class after that."

At seventeen, Musk left South Africa for Canada. Musk wanted to get to the United States as quickly as possible, and he could use Canada to get to the United States because his mom's parents were from there. He figured Canada might serve as a gateway for getting to Silicon Valley.

As soon as a law had passed allowing Maye to pass her Canadian citizenship to her children, Elon plotted his escape. Musk immediately began figuring out how to complete the paperwork to become a Canadian citizen on his own. It took about a year to be approved and get a Canadian passport. "That's when Elon said, 'I'm leaving for Canada,'" Maye said. In those pre-internet days, Musk had to wait three long weeks to get a plane ticket. Once it arrived, and without flinching, he left home for good.

4

AN AWAKENING IN CANADA

MUSK DID NOT PLAN HIS great escape to Canada well. He knew of a great-uncle in Montreal, hopped on a flight, and hoped for the best. When he landed in June of 1989, Musk found a pay phone and tried to use directory assistance to find his uncle. When that didn't work, he called his mother collect to ask for suggestions.

She had bad news. Maye had sent a letter to the uncle before Musk left and received a reply while her son was traveling. The uncle had gone to Minnesota, meaning Musk had nowhere to stay. Bags in hand, Musk headed for a youth hostel, an inexpensive hotel for young adults.

After spending a few days in Montreal exploring the city, Musk tried to find more permanent accommodations. Maye had family scattered all across Canada, and Musk began reaching out to them. He bought a countrywide bus ticket that let him hop on and off buses as he pleased. He then headed to Saskatchewan, the province where his grandfather had lived.

After the long bus ride, he ended up in the small town of Swift Current. Elon called a cousin out of the blue from the bus station. He then hitchhiked to his house.

Musk started doing some work on his cousin's farm. He grew vegetables and shoveled out grain bins. Musk celebrated his eighteenth birthday there, sharing a cake with the family. Throughout the rest of the year, Musk hopped from city to city, working odd jobs. At one point, for example, he learned to cut logs with a chainsaw in Vancouver, British Columbia.

Musk found some of his jobs by going to the local employment offices where companies posted requests for work. He was told that the best-paying job—because of the hazards involved—was cleaning boilers at a lumber mill, so he decided to try that. "You have to put on this hazmat suit and then shimmy through this little tunnel that you can barely fit in," Musk said. "Then you have a shovel and you take the sand and goop and other residue, which is still steaming hot, and you have to shovel it through the same hole you came through. There is no escape. Someone else on the other side has to shovel it into a wheelbarrow. If you stay in there for more than thirty minutes, you get too hot and die." Thirty people started out at the beginning of the week to give the job a try. By the end of the week, it was just Musk and two other men doing the work.

As Musk made his way around Canada, his brother, sister, and mother were figuring out how to get there as well. Maye went to Canada to look at possible places to live. While she was there, Tosca, then fourteen, put the family house in South Africa and all their furniture up for sale. She also sold Maye's car. When Maye got back and asked Tosca why she was selling all of Maye's possessions, Tosca answered, "We are getting out of here."

After Elon's family settled down in Canada, Musk enrolled at Queen's University in Kingston, Ontario. When not at school, Elon would read the newspaper with Kimbal. The two of them would identify interesting people they would like to meet. They then took turns cold-calling these people to ask if they would be willing to have lunch.

Musk ran away to Canada and ended up at Queen's University in Ontario, living in a dormitory for foreign students. © Maye Musk

One of the men they called was Peter Nicholson, a top executive at the Bank of Nova Scotia. Nicholson remembered the boys' call well. "I was not in the habit of getting out-of-the-blue requests," he said. "I was perfectly prepared to have lunch with a couple of kids that had that kind of gumption." It took six months to get on Nicholson's calendar, but, sure enough, the Musk brothers made a three-hour train ride and showed up on time.

Nicholson's first impression of the Musk brothers was that both were polite. Elon seemed the geekier, more awkward brother, while Kimbal was charismatic and personable. "I became more impressed and fascinated as I talked to them," Nicholson said. "They were so determined." Nicholson ended up offering Elon a summer internship at the bank.

Not long after, Elon invited Peter Nicholson's daughter Christie to another one of his birthday parties. Elon had never met Christie before, but he went right up to her at the party and led her to a couch. "Then, I believe the second sentence out of his mouth was, 'I think a lot about electric cars,'" Christie said. "And then he turned to me and said, 'Do you think about electric cars?'"

Christie knew immediately that Elon was different and found him interesting. The two would later have long conversations on the phone. During one of these, Elon said, "If there was a way that I could not eat, so I could work more, I would not eat. I wish there was a way to get nutrients without sitting down for a meal." Christie was struck by the idea that anyone would be so consumed by the desire to work that they would perhaps do without food.

While Elon was at Queen's, he also met Justine Wilson, another student there. She was smart and pretty, with long, brown hair and a black belt in tae kwon do. Elon liked her a lot, but he wasn't really her type. She had been looking more for a boy with a wild side than an awkward science geek. Musk, though, persisted, bringing Justine ice cream while she studied and inviting her to parties, and they eventually began dating.

Musk liked college. His know-it-all ways were received better by the college students. Musk found a group of friends who respected his intellectual abilities and enjoyed the challenge of school. The university students didn't make fun of his opinions on energy, space, and whatever else he was thinking about at the time. People liked his ambition, and he thrived in this environment.

Navaid Farooq, a Canadian who grew up abroad, ended up in Musk's dormitory in the fall of 1990, and the two men hit it off. They shared an interest in strategy board games. When the video game Civilization was released, the two friends spent hours building their empire. "I don't think he makes friends easily, but he is very loyal to those he has," Farooq said.

For a time, Musk sold computer parts and full PCs in the dorm to make some extra cash. "I could build something to suit their needs, like a tricked-out gaming machine or a simple word processor that cost less than what they could get in a store," Musk said. "Or if their computer didn't boot properly or had a virus, I'd fix it. I could pretty much solve any problem."

Musk was more ambitious in college than he'd been in

high school. He studied business and competed in public speaking contests. He also began to display the intensity and competitiveness that mark his behavior today. "When Elon gets into something, he develops just this different level of interest in it than other people," Farooq said. "That is what differentiates Elon from the rest of humanity."

In 1992, after two years at Queen's, Musk transferred to the University of Pennsylvania on a scholarship. Musk saw the Ivy League school as opening up more opportunities and went off in pursuit of dual degrees—first an economics degree from the Wharton School and then a bachelor's degree in physics. Justine stayed at Queen's, but she and Musk still dated long-distance.

Musk blossomed even more at Penn, and really started to feel comfortable while hanging out with his fellow physics students. "At Penn, he met people that thought like him," Maye said. "There were some nerds there. He so enjoyed them. I remember going for lunch with them, and they were talking physics things. They were saying, 'A plus B equals pi squared' or whatever. They would laugh out loud. It was cool to see him so happy." Musk did make one very close friend, named Adeo Ressi, who would go on to be a Silicon Valley businessman in his own right and is to this day as tight with Elon as anyone.

Ressi is a lanky guy well over six feet tall. He was much more artistic than the studious, serious Musk. Both of the young men were transfer students and ended up renting a large house away from the main campus. They got the ten-bedroom home relatively cheap, since it was a fraternity house that had gone unrented. During the week, Musk and Ressi would study, but as the weekend approached, Ressi, in particular, would transform the house into a nightclub. He covered the windows with trash bags to make it pitch-black inside and decorated the walls with bright paints and whatever objects he could find. They would charge $5 for entry to the parties and get as many as five hundred people to show up.

A second house they rented later had fourteen rooms. Musk, Ressi, and one other person lived there. Musk returned home one day to find that Ressi had nailed his desk to the wall and then painted it in Day-Glo colors. Musk pulled down the desk, painted it black, and began studying. "I'm like, 'Dude, that's installation art in our party house,'" said Ressi. But, to Musk, it was a desk.

While Musk didn't do a lot to set up the parties, he was the one who ran them. "I was paying my own way through college and could make an entire month's rent in one night," he said. As Ressi put it, "Elon was the most straitlaced dude you have ever met. He never did anything. Zero. Literally nothing." Musk studied maniacally and kept on playing video games. Sometimes Ressi had to step in and stop Musk from playing, during game binges that could go on for days.

Musk's longtime interest in solar power and in finding other new ways to harness energy expanded at Penn. In December 1994, he wrote a paper titled "The Importance of Being Solar." The document started with a bit of Musk's wry sense of humor. At the top of the page, he wrote: "'The sun will come out tomorrow . . .'—Little Orphan Annie on the subject of renewable energy." The paper went on to predict a rise in solar power technology, and Musk received a 98 percent on what his professor deemed a "very interesting and well-written paper."

As Musk began to think more seriously about what he would do after college, he briefly considered getting into the video game business. He'd loved video games since his childhood and had held a gaming internship. But he came to see them as not quite worthwhile enough. "I really like computer games, but then if I made really great computer games, how much effect would that have on the world?" he said. "It wouldn't have a big effect. Even though I have an intrinsic love of video games, I couldn't bring myself to do that as a career."

According to Musk, he was never interested in just making money. Even in college, he was thinking about what humans need. "I'm not an investor," he said. "I like to make technologies real that I think are important for the future and useful in some sort of way."

5

ELON'S FIRST START-UP

IN THE SUMMER OF 1994, Musk and his brother, Kimbal, set off on a road trip across the United States.

In a beat-up 1970s BMW, the brothers began their journey near San Francisco. It was August, and the temperatures in California were soaring. The first part of the drive took them down to the Mojave Desert. There, they experienced the sweaty thrill of 120-degree weather in a car with no air-conditioning. They learned to love stops at Carl's Jr. burger joints, where they spent hours recovering in the cold air-conditioning.

The trip provided plenty of time for your typical twenty-something adventures and daydreams about business. The internet had just started to become really popular, and the brothers thought they might like to start a company together doing something on the web. They took turns driving and talking before heading back east to get Musk to school that fall, but they didn't love any of their ideas for a business.

Musk had spent the earlier part of that summer in Silicon Valley, holding down a pair of internships. By day, he worked at the start-up Pinnacle Research Institute. There, scientists explored ways in which a type of device that stores energy called an ultracapacitor could be used as a fuel source, possibly in electric and hybrid vehicles.

The work also veered into more bizarre territory. Musk could talk at length about how ultracapacitors might be used to build laser guns in the tradition of *Star Wars*. The guns would release rounds of enormous energy, and then the shooter would replace an ultracapacitor at the base of the gun, and start blasting away again. Musk fell in love with the work at Pinnacle.

In the evenings, Musk headed to Rocket Science Games, a new business that wanted to create the most advanced video games ever made by moving them off cartridges and onto CDs. The CDs would hold more information and could possibly allow for movie-quality graphics and storytelling.

A team of all-star engineers and film people was assembled to make the games. People worked at the office twenty-four hours a day, and they didn't think it was weird that Musk would turn up around five every evening to start his second job. He was brought in to write some easy software code but, very shortly, assigned himself more challenging tasks. According to Peter Barrett, an Australian engineer who helped start the company, "I don't think anyone was giving him any direction, and he ended up making what he wanted to make."

Musk found in Silicon Valley the opportunity he'd been seeking his entire life and a place equal to his ambitions. He would return two summers in a row and then permanently after graduating with dual degrees from Penn. He initially intended to get an advanced degree in physics from Stanford University, focusing on developing the ultracapacitors. As the story goes, Musk dropped out of Stanford after two days, finding the internet's call and the prospect of starting a business irresistible. He talked Kimbal into moving to Silicon Valley as well so they could conquer the web together.

The idea for their internet business had come to Musk during his internships. A salesperson from the Yellow Pages had come into one of the offices. The salesperson tried to sell the idea of an online listing to complement the regular listing a company would have in the big, fat Yellow Pages book. The salesman clearly had little understanding of what the internet actually was. The bad sales pitch got

Musk thinking. So he reached out to Kimbal with the idea of helping businesses get online for the first time.

"Elon said, 'These guys don't know what they are talking about. Maybe this is something we can do,'" Kimbal said. This was 1995, and the brothers were about to form Global Link Information Network, a start-up that would eventually be renamed Zip2.

The Zip2 idea was ingenious. Few small businesses in 1995 understood the internet because it was such a new concept. They had little idea how to get on it and didn't really see the value in creating a website for their business or even in having a listing online that potential customers could find. Musk and his brother hoped to convince restaurants, hairdressers, and the like that the time had come for them to make their presence known to the web-surfing public. Zip2 would create a searchable directory of businesses and tie this into maps. Musk often explained the concept through pizza, saying that everyone deserved the right to know the location of their closest pizza parlor and the turn-by-turn directions to get there. This may seem obvious today—think Yelp meets Google Maps—but it was not obvious back then.

The Musk brothers rented a tiny office not far from Stanford in Palo Alto, California, and acquired some basic furniture. The three-story building had no elevators, and the toilets often didn't work.

Musk, then twenty-three years old, did all of the original coding for Zip2 himself, while Kimbal looked to start the door-to-door sales operations. Musk managed to acquire access to a database of business listings in the Bay Area that would give a business's name and address. He then acquired the use of some digital maps and directions and merged all of the technology together to create the service.

Errol Musk gave his sons $28,000 to help them through this period, but they were more or less broke after getting the office space, licensing software, and buying some equipment. For the first three months of Zip2's life, Musk and his brother lived at the office. They had a small closet where they kept their clothes and would shower at the YMCA. "Sometimes we ate four meals a day at Jack in the Box," Kimbal said. "It was open twenty-four hours, which suited our work schedule. I haven't been able to eat there since, but I can still recite their menu."

Zip2 may have been an internet business, but getting it started required old-fashioned door-to-door salesmanship. Businesses needed to be persuaded of the web's benefits and charmed into paying for the unknown.

In late 1995, the Musk brothers began making their first hires and assembling a motley sales team. Jeff Heilman, a free-spirited twenty-year-old trying to figure out what to do with his life, arrived as one of Zip2's first recruits. A handful of other salespeople joined him and worked for a commission—or a portion of the money they were able to bring in from a business.

Musk never seemed to leave the office. He slept, not unlike a dog, on a beanbag next to his desk. "Almost every day, I'd come in at seven thirty or eight a.m., and he'd be asleep right there on that bag," Heilman said. "Maybe he showered on the weekends. I don't know." Musk asked those first employees of Zip2 to give him a kick when they arrived, and he'd wake up and get back to work.

While Musk did his coder thing, Kimbal became the sales leader. "Kimbal was the eternal optimist, and he was very, very uplifting," Heilman said. Kimbal sent Heilman to the high-end shops of Palo Alto to convince the managers to sign up with Zip2.

The big problem, of course, was that no one was buying. Week after week, Heilman knocked on doors and returned to the office with very little good news to report. When lunchtime came around, the Musks would reach into a cigar box where they kept some cash, take Heilman out, and get the depressing reports on the sales.

Craig Mohr, another early employee, gave up his job selling real estate to hawk Zip2's service. He decided to focus on convincing car dealerships to try Zip2 because they usually spent lots of money on advertising. "One day

I came back with about nine hundred dollars in checks," Mohr said. "I walked into the office and asked the guys what they wanted me to do with the money. Elon stopped pounding his keyboard, leaned out from behind his monitor, and said, 'No way, you've got money.'"

Greg Kouri, a Canadian businessman in his midthirties, also joined Zip2. He had met the Musks in Toronto and liked the idea of Zip2. The boys had showed up at his door one morning to inform Kouri that they intended to head to California to give the business a shot. Still in his bathrobe, Kouri went back into the house, dug around for a couple of minutes, and came back with a wad of $6,000 to invest in the company. In early 1996, he moved to California and became a cofounder of Zip2.

Kouri had actual business experience and read people well. He, therefore, served as the adult supervision at Zip2. The Canadian had a knack for calming Musk and ended up becoming something of a mentor. "Really smart people sometimes don't understand that not everyone can keep up with them or go as fast," said Derek Proudian, who would become Zip2's chief executive officer (CEO). "Greg is one of the few people that Elon would listen to." Kouri also used to referee fistfights between Elon and Kimbal that broke out in the middle of the office.

"I don't get in fights with anyone else, but Elon and

I don't have the ability to reconcile a vision other than our own," Kimbal said. During a particularly nasty scrap over a business decision, Elon ripped some skin off his fist and had to go get a tetanus shot. Kouri put an end to the fights after that.

In early 1996, Zip2 underwent a massive change. The venture capital firm Mohr Davidow Ventures regularly gave new businesses large amounts of money in exchange for owning part of the company. Mohr Davidow had heard of a couple of South African boys trying to make a Yellow Pages for the internet and met with the brothers. The investors came away impressed with Musk's energy.

Mohr Davidow invested $3 million into the company. With this money in hand, the company officially changed its name from Global Link to Zip2—the idea being zip to here, zip to there. It also moved to a larger office and began hiring talented engineers.

Zip2 shifted its business idea as well. At the time, the company had built one of the best direction systems on the web. Zip2 would improve this technology and take it from focusing just on the Bay Area to covering other major cities in the United States. Then, instead of selling its service door-to-door, Zip2 would create a software package that could be sold to newspapers, which would in turn build their own directories.

Musk did not like the change in the business focus or how the company was run. The investors pushed Musk into the role of chief technology officer, so he was now in charge of the technology, but no longer ran the company. Instead, they hired someone else as the company's chief executive officer.

While Musk had excelled as a coder who had taught himself, his skills weren't as polished as those of the new hires. They took one look at Zip2's code and began rewriting the software to clean it up.

The engineers also set more realistic deadlines. This was a welcome change from Musk's approach, which had been to set very tight deadlines and then try to get engineers to work nonstop for days on end to meet the goals. "If you asked Elon how long it would take to do something, there was never anything in his mind that would take more than an hour," said one Zip2 employee. "We came to interpret an hour as really taking a day or two."

Starting Zip2 and watching it grow gave Musk self-confidence. One of Musk's high school friends came to California for a visit and noticed the change in Musk's character right away. He watched Musk confront a nasty landlord who had been giving his mother a hard time. Musk said, "If you're going to bully someone, bully me." In high school, Elon had been the kid people picked on to get a response. Now he was confident and in control.

Zip2 had remarkable success selling to newspapers. The newspapers had been slow to build their own internet services, and Zip2 gave them a way to sell cars and other things to their readers. In 1997, Zip2 moved into a nicer office in the nearby city of Mountain View.

It bothered Musk that Zip2 had started selling only to newspapers. He believed the company could offer interesting services directly to everybody. He encouraged Zip2 to buy the domain name "city.com" with the hopes of turning it into a site for the public. But the CEO of Zip2 decided it was better to continue focusing on newspapers.

In April 1998, Zip2 announced that it would merge with its main competitor, Citysearch. Musk liked the idea of the merger at first but then turned against it. In May 1998, the two companies canceled the merger, which caused a lot of tumult inside of Zip2.

With the deal busted, Zip2 had a problem. The company had done well, but it was losing money as it tried to build out its service and hire lots of salespeople. Musk still wanted to focus on offering Zip2 to everyone, but a new CEO feared that expanding the service and building more technology would take too much money. While Musk and others debated the future of Zip2, more competitors arrived offering similar things. The internet had become extremely popular, and plenty of people were trying to build online businesses.

Then, in February 1999, the large PC maker Compaq suddenly offered to pay $307 million in cash for Zip2. "It was like pennies from heaven," said Ed Ho, a former Zip2 employee. Zip2 accepted the offer and threw a huge party. Mohr Davidow had made back twenty times its original investment, and Musk had come away with $22 million. Musk never thought about sticking around to work at Compaq. As soon as he knew the company would be sold, he was on to something else.

Musk had learned a major lesson from Zip2, mostly that he would not let investors exert too much influence over his ventures. From that point on, Musk would fight to keep control of his companies and stay CEO. "We were overwhelmed and just thought, 'These guys must know what they're doing,'" Kimbal said. "But they didn't. There was no vision once they took over."

Years later, after he had time to think about the Zip2 situation, Musk realized that he could have handled some of the interactions with employees better. Musk had sometimes berated people during meetings and asked his employees to work very long hours. "I had never really run a team of any sort before," Musk said. "I'd never been a sports captain or a captain of anything or managed a single person. You have to put yourself in a position where you say, 'Well, how would this sound to them, knowing what they know?'"

Musk tells the story of one guy who wrote an incorrect equation on a board at Zip2. "I'm like, 'How can you write that?'" Musk said. "Then I corrected it for him. He hated me after that." Musk had embarrassed the employee in front of lots of people at the company. "Eventually, I realized, okay, I might have fixed that thing, but now I've made the person unproductive. It just wasn't a good way to go about things."

With Zip2, Musk had been both lucky and good. He had a decent idea, turned it into a real service, and came out of the dot-com craziness with cash in his pockets. That was better than what most people could say. The process, however, had been painful. Musk had wanted to be a leader, but the people around him didn't see how Musk as the CEO could work. As far as Musk was concerned, they were all wrong. He then set out to prove it.

6

THE PAYPAL YEARS

MUCH LIKE THE VIDEO GAME characters he adored, Musk had leveled up. He had solved Silicon Valley and become what everyone at the time wanted to be—a dot-com millionaire. But that was not good enough for Musk, and he had quickly started thinking about his next move. Ever ambitious, Musk knew that his next venture would need to be even bigger than Zip2. This left him searching for a huge industry that could be challenged and improved.

Musk began thinking back to his time as an intern at the Bank of Nova Scotia. There, he had formed the opinion that many bankers are rich but not too bright—which now felt like an opportunity.

For years, Musk had been considering starting an

internet bank. He had even discussed it openly during his internship at Pinnacle Research in 1995. Musk had lectured the scientists about the transition coming in finance where people would stop visiting local banks and start doing most of their banking online. The scientists tried to talk him down, saying that it would take ages for web security to be good enough to handle online transactions safely. Musk, though, remained convinced that the finance industry could do with a major upgrade.

The actual plan that Musk concocted was beyond ambitious. As the researchers at Pinnacle had pointed out, people were barely comfortable buying books online. They might take their chances entering a credit card number, but exposing their bank accounts to the web was out of the question. Pah. So what? Musk wanted to build a full-service bank online: a company that would have savings and checking accounts as well as brokerage services and insurance.

The technology to build such a service was possible, but figuring out the complex laws of creating an online bank from scratch looked impossible. This was not dishing out directions to a pizzeria or putting up a listing for a used car. It was dealing with people's finances, and there would be huge consequences if the service did not work as billed.

Bold as ever, Musk kicked this new plan into action

before Zip2 had even been sold. He chatted up some of the best engineers at Zip2 to get a feel for who might be willing to join him in another venture. Musk also bounced his ideas off some contacts he'd made at the bank in Canada. In January 1999, with Zip2's board seeking a buyer, Musk began to polish his banking plan. The deal with Compaq was announced the next month, and in March, Musk incorporated X.com, his new start-up.

It had taken Musk less than a decade to go from being a Canadian backpacker to becoming a multimillionaire at the age of twenty-seven. With his $22 million, he moved from sharing an apartment with three roommates to buying an 1,800-square-foot condo and renovating it. He also bought a $1 million McLaren F1 sports car and, perhaps inspired by his grandfather, a small plane, which he learned to fly.

While he enjoyed playing with his new toys, Musk remained focused on reserving most of his newfound wealth to fund his business ideas. To his credit, Musk plowed the majority of the money he made from Zip2 straight into X.com. Even by Silicon Valley's high-risk standards, it was shocking to put so much of one's wealth into something as iffy as an online bank. All told, Musk invested about $12 million into X.com, leaving him, after taxes, with $4 million or so for personal use. "That's part of what separates Elon from mere mortals," said Ed Ho, the former Zip2 executive who went on to cofound X.com. "He's willing to take an insane amount of personal risk. When you do a deal like that, it either pays off or you end up in a bus shelter somewhere."

Musk's decision to invest so much money in X.com looks even more unusual in hindsight. Much of the point of being a dot-com success in 1999 was to prove yourself once, stash away your millions, and then talk other people into betting their money on your next company. Musk would certainly go on to rely on outside investors, but he took on a lot of personal risk as well. In that way, Musk behaved more like Silicon Valley's earlier founders, when the starters of companies like chip maker Intel were willing to take huge gambles on themselves.

Where Zip2 had been a neat, useful idea, X.com held the promise of starting a major revolution. Musk, for the first time, would be going against a wealthy, established industry with the hopes of beating many very powerful companies. Musk did not let the fact that he knew very little about the complex details of banking bother him. He had an idea that the bankers were doing finance all wrong—being too slow and too old-fashioned—and that he could run the business better than everyone else.

Musk assembled what looked like an all-star crew to start X.com. There were four founders, and they all agreed that the banking industry had fallen behind the times.

Despite their shared vision and enthusiasm, however, the group soon ran into problems. It proved very difficult to navigate the complex banking laws and to modernize an industry that fought change.

Just five months after X.com started, one of the cofounders, Harris Fricker, decided that X.com needed new leadership. "He said either he takes over as CEO or he's just going to take everyone from the company and create his own company," Musk said. "I don't do well with blackmail. I said, 'You should go do that.' So he did."

Musk tried to talk some of the other key engineers into staying, but they sided with Fricker and left. Musk ended up with a shell of a company and a handful of loyal employees. "After all that went down, I remember sitting with Elon in his office," said Julie Ankenbrandt, an early X.com employee who stayed. "There were a million laws in place to block something like X.com from happening, but Elon didn't care. He just looked at me and said, 'I guess we should hire some more people.'"

Musk had been trying to raise funding for X.com and had had to go to the investors and confess that there wasn't much in the way of a company left. Mike Moritz, a famed investor from Sequoia Capital, backed the company nonetheless, making a bet on Musk and little else. Musk hit the streets of Silicon Valley once again and managed to attract engineers with his rah-rah speeches about the glorious future of internet banking and his plans to make people's lives easier.

Week by week, more engineers arrived, and the vision became more real. The company secured a banking license and licenses to deal in other financial products. By November, X.com's small software team had created one of the world's first online banks, complete with government-approved insurance to back the bank accounts and three investment funds for people to choose.

Under Musk's direction, X.com tried out some crazy new banking ideas. Customers received a twenty-dollar cash card just for signing up to use the bank and a ten-dollar card for every person they referred to the service. X.com also built a person-to-person payment system in which you could send someone money just by plugging their email address into the site. The whole idea was to shift away from slow-moving banks that took days to process payments and create a kind of quick bank account where you could move money around with a couple of clicks on a mouse. This was revolutionary stuff, and more than two hundred thousand people signed up for X.com within the first couple of months of operation.

Soon enough, X.com had a major competitor. A couple of brainy kids named Max Levchin and Peter Thiel had been working on a payment system of their own at their start-up called Confinity. The duo actually rented their office space—a glorified broom closet—from X.com and were trying to make it possible for owners of PalmPilot handhelds to swap money via the infrared ports on the devices. Between X.com and Confinity, the small office in Palo Alto had turned into the center of the internet finance revolution. "It was this mass of adolescent men that worked so hard," Ankenbrandt said. "It stunk so badly in there. I can still smell it—leftover pizza, body odor, and sweat."

The pleasantries between X.com and Confinity came to an abrupt end. The Confinity founders moved to an office down the street and, like X.com, began focusing their attention on web-based payments with their service known as PayPal. The companies became locked in a heated battle to match each other's features and attract more users, knowing that whoever got bigger faster would win. Tens of millions of dollars were spent on promotions, while millions more were lost battling hackers who had seized upon the services as new opportunities for fraud. "You gave away money as fast as you could," described Jeremy Stoppelman, an X.com engineer who went on to become the CEO of Yelp.

In March 2000, X.com and Confinity finally decided to stop trying to spend each other into oblivion and to join forces through a merger. The merger left Musk as the largest shareholder of the combined company, which would be called X.com. Shortly after the deal closed, X.com raised $100 million from backers and boasted that it had more than one million customers.

X.com had been battling fraud and other computer issues, and these problems worsened as the company's computing systems failed to keep up with a rapidly growing customer base. Once a week, the company's website collapsed. Most of the engineers were ordered to start work designing a new system, which distracted key technical personnel and left X.com vulnerable to fraud.

"We were losing money hand over fist," said Stoppelman. As X.com became more popular, all of its problems worsened. There was more fraud. There were more fees from banks and credit card companies. There was more competition from other start-ups. X.com lacked a cohesive business model to offset the losses and turn a profit from the money it managed. A growing number of people at the company questioned Musk's decision-making.

What followed was one of the nastiest overthrows in Silicon Valley's long history of nasty overthrows. A small group of X.com employees gathered one night and brainstormed about how to push out Musk. They decided to sell the company's board of directors on the idea of Peter Thiel, who had cofounded Confinity, returning as CEO. Instead of confronting Musk directly with this plan, the conspirators decided to take action behind Musk's back.

Musk and Justine had been married in January 2000 but had been too busy for a honeymoon. Nine months later, in September, they planned to mix business and pleasure by going on a fund-raising trip for the company and ending it with a honeymoon in Sydney, Australia, to catch the Olympics. As they boarded their flight one night, X.com executives delivered letters to X.com's board urging the directors to replace Musk.

Some of the people loyal to Musk had sensed something was wrong, but it was too late. "I went to the office at ten thirty that night, and everyone was there," Ankenbrandt said. "I could not believe it. I am frantically trying to call Elon, but he's on a plane." By the time he landed, Musk had been replaced by Thiel.

When Musk finally heard what had happened, he hopped on the next plane back to Palo Alto. For a brief period, Musk tried to fight for his job. He urged the board to reconsider its decision. But when it became clear that the company had already moved on, Musk relented. He said, "It wasn't so much that I wanted to be CEO but more like, 'Hey, I think there are some pretty important things that need to happen, and if I'm not CEO, I'm not sure they are going to happen.'" Musk talked to Thiel and felt better after their discussion, thinking Thiel would act on some of his suggestions for the company.

By June 2001, Musk's influence on the company was fading quickly. That month, Thiel rebranded X.com as PayPal. Musk embraced the role of being an advisor to the company and kept investing in it, increasing his stake as PayPal's largest shareholder. "You would expect someone in Elon's position to be bitter and vindictive, but he wasn't," said PayPal's former chief financial officer Roelof Botha. "He supported Peter. He was a prince."

The next few months would end up being key for Musk's future. The dot-com joyride was coming to a quick end, and people wanted to try and cash out in any way possible. When executives from eBay began approaching PayPal about purchasing it, most people wanted to sell and sell fast.

Musk, though, urged the board to reject a number of offers and hold out for more money. PayPal had revenue of about $240 million per year, and looked like it might survive as a company. Musk's resistance paid off and then some. In July 2002, eBay offered $1.5 billion for PayPal, and Musk and the rest of the board accepted the deal. Musk made about $250 million from the sale to eBay, or $180 million after taxes—enough to make what would turn out to be his very wild dreams possible.

7

MICE IN SPACE

ELON TURNED THIRTY IN JUNE 2001, a little more than a year before eBay offered to buy PayPal. That birthday hit him hard. "I'm no longer a child prodigy," he told Justine, only half joking. That same month X.com officially changed its name to PayPal, providing a harsh reminder that the company had been ripped away from Musk and given to someone else to run. The start-up life had gotten old, and so had Silicon Valley.

The idea of escaping started to grow more and more appealing. Elon and Justine decided to move south and begin their family and the next chapter of their lives in Los Angeles, even while Elon still acted as an advisor for PayPal.

"There's an element to him that likes the style and the

excitement and color of a place like LA," said Justine. "Elon likes to be where the action is." A small group of Musk's friends who felt similarly had also moved to Los Angeles.

But, it wasn't just Los Angeles's glitz that attracted Musk. It was also the call of space. After being pushed out of PayPal, Musk had started to remember his childhood fantasies about rocket ships and space travel. He started to think that he might be destined for bigger things than just creating internet services.

Musk had picked Los Angeles on purpose. It gave him access to space, or at least the space industry. Southern California's mild, consistent weather had made it a favored city of the aeronautics industry since the 1920s, when the Lockheed Aircraft Service Company set up shop in Holly-wood. Howard Hughes, the US Air Force, NASA, Boeing, and many other people and organizations have performed much of their manufacturing and cutting-edge experimen-tation in and around Los Angeles.

While Musk didn't know exactly what he wanted to do in space, he knew that just by being in Los Angeles he would be surrounded by the world's top space thinkers. They could help him perfect any ideas, and there would be plenty of recruits to join his next business.

Musk's first interactions with the space community were with members of a nonprofit group called the Mars

Society. The Mars Society was dedicated to exploring and settling Mars, and it planned to hold a fund-raiser in mid-2001. The $500-per-plate event was to take place at the house of one of the wealthy Mars Society members, and invitations to the usual characters had been mailed out.

What stunned Robert Zubrin, the head of the group, was a reply from someone named Elon Musk, whom no one could remember inviting. "He gave us a check for five thousand dollars," Zubrin said. "That made everyone take notice." Zubrin began researching Musk, determined he was rich, and invited him for coffee ahead of the dinner. "I wanted to make sure he knew the projects we had under way," Zubrin said.

When they met, Zubrin began to tell Musk about the research center the society had built in the Arctic to mimic the tough conditions of Mars. Zubrin also told Elon about the experiments the society had been running for something called the Translife Mission, in which there would be a spinning capsule orbiting Earth that was piloted by a crew of mice. "It would spin to give them one-third gravity—the same you would have on Mars—and they would live there and reproduce," Zubrin told Musk.

When it was time for the dinner, Zubrin placed Musk at the VIP table next to himself, the film director and space buff James Cameron, and Carol Stoker, a planetary scientist for NASA. "Elon is so youthful-looking, and at that time he looked like a little boy," Stoker said. "Cameron was chatting him up right away to invest in his next movie, and Zubrin was trying to get him to make a big donation to the Mars Society."

Musk, meanwhile, probed about for ideas and contacts. Stoker's husband was an aerospace engineer at NASA, working on a concept for an airplane that would glide over Mars looking for water. Musk loved that. "He was much more intense than some of the other millionaires," Zubrin said. "He didn't know a lot about space, but he had a scientific mind. He wanted to know exactly what was being planned in regards to Mars and what the significance would be." Musk took to the Mars Society right away and joined its board of directors. He donated another $100,000 to fund a research station in the desert as well.

Musk's friends were not entirely sure what to make of his mental state. With little prompting, Musk would start talking about his desire to do something meaningful with his life—something lasting. Musk had actually started thinking bigger than the Mars Society. Rather than send a few mice into Earth's orbit, Musk wanted to send them to Mars.

The more Musk thought about space, the more important its exploration seemed to him. He felt as if the public had lost some of its ambition and hope for the future. The average person might see space exploration as a waste of time and effort, but Musk thought about interplanetary travel in a very serious way. He wanted to inspire the masses and reignite their passion for science, conquest, and the promise of technology.

Musk believed that the very idea of America was intertwined with humanity's desire to explore. He found it sad that NASA, the American agency tasked with doing fantastic things in space and exploring new frontiers, seemed to have no serious interest in investigating Mars at all.

Musk began to set up meetings with his new contacts in the space industry in hotel conference rooms. He mostly wanted them to help him develop the mice-to-Mars idea or at least to come up with something similar. Musk hoped to hit on a grand gesture for mankind—some type of event that would capture the world's attention, get people thinking about Mars again, and about man's potential. He resigned from his position as a director of the Mars Society and announced his own organization—the Life to Mars Foundation.

The experts were thrilled to have another rich guy appear who was willing to pay for something interesting in space. They happily debated sending up mice. But, as the discussions wore on, the interest turned toward a different project—something called Mars Oasis. Under this plan,

Musk would buy a rocket and use it to shoot what amounted to a robotic greenhouse to Mars. A group of researchers had already been working on a space-ready growth chamber for plants. The idea was to modify their structure so that it could open up briefly and suck in some of the Martian soil and then use it to grow a plant, which would in turn produce the first oxygen on Mars. Much to Musk's liking, this new plan seemed both grand and achievable.

Musk wanted the structure to have a window and a way to send a video feedback to Earth so that people could watch the plant grow. The group also talked about sending out kits to students around the country, who would grow their own plants simultaneously and take notice, for example, that the Martian plant could grow twice as high as its Earthbound counterpart in the same amount of time.

The main thing troubling the space experts was Musk's budget. It seemed like Musk wanted to spend somewhere between $20 million and $30 million on the stunt. Everyone knew that the cost of a rocket launch alone would eat up that money and then some. "In my mind, you needed $200 million to do it right," said one aerospace whiz who attended the meetings.

Musk turned some of the volunteer thinkers into consultants and put them to work on the plant machine's design. He also planned a trip to Russia to find out exactly how much a launch would cost. Musk intended to buy a refurbished intercontinental ballistic missile, or ICBM, from the Russians and use that as his launch vehicle. For help with this, Musk reached out to Jim Cantrell, an unusual fellow who had done work for the United States and other governments. Cantrell had been accused of espionage by the Russians and placed under house arrest in 1996 after a satellite deal did not go well. "After a couple of weeks, Al Gore [the former vice president] made some calls, and it got worked out," Cantrell said. "I didn't want anything to do with the Russians again—ever." Musk had other ideas.

When Musk and Cantrell finally met, they really hit it off. Musk rolled out his "humans need to become a multiplanetary species" speech, urging that humans must have a major backup plan in case something goes terribly wrong on Earth. Cantrell said that if Musk was really serious, he'd be willing to go to Russia—again—and help buy a rocket.

In late October 2001, Musk, Cantrell, and Adeo Ressi, Musk's friend from college, boarded a commercial flight to Moscow. Ressi had been trying to figure out whether his best friend had started to lose his mind, and along with some other of Musk's friends, tried to talk him out of wasting his money on space experiments. When Ressi couldn't change Musk's mind, he went along to Russia to try to watch out for Musk as best as he could.

"Adeo would call me to the side and say, 'What Elon is doing is insane. A philanthropic gesture? That's crazy,'" Cantrell said. "He was seriously worried but was down with the trip." And why not? The men were heading to Russia, where rich guys could apparently buy space missiles on the open market.

Team Musk would grow to include Mike Griffin, who had degrees in aerospace engineering, electrical engineering, civil engineering, and applied physics. He had worked for various technology and launch companies and at Jet Propulsion Laboratory (JPL), which develops and builds robotic spacecraft. Some would say that no one on the planet knew more about the realities of getting things into space than Griffin. In 2005 he would take over as head of NASA, but four years earlier, he was going to Russia with Musk.

The group met with the Russians three times over a period of four months, but the meetings did not go well. The Russians spent long hours eating and making small talk before they would get down to business. Even then, they did not seem to take Elon seriously. "They looked at us like we were not credible people," Cantrell said, and then described how one of their chief designers spit on him and Elon because he thought they didn't really intend to buy the missiles.

The most intense meeting occurred in a once-fancy building near downtown Moscow. Musk sat on $20 million, which he hoped would be enough to buy three ICBMs that could be retooled to go to space. The Russians were again refusing to get down to business, and so Musk finally asked point-blank how much a missile would cost. The reply: $8 million each. Musk countered, offering $8 million for two. "They sat there and looked at him," Cantrell said. "And said something like, 'Young boy. No.' They also intimated that he didn't have the money." At this point, Musk had decided the Russians were either not serious about doing business or determined to part a dot-com millionaire from as much of his money as possible. He walked out of the meeting.

The Team Musk mood could not have been worse. It was near the end of February 2002, and they went outside to hail a cab and drove straight to the airport in the midst of a snowstorm. Inside the cab, no one talked. Musk had come to Russia filled with optimism about putting on a great show for mankind and was now leaving disappointed by human nature. The Russians were the only ones with rockets that could possibly fit within Musk's budget.

The somber mood lingered all the way to the plane. "You always feel particularly good when the wheels lift off in Moscow," Cantrell said. "It's like, 'My God. I made it.'" Musk sat in the row in front of them, typing on his computer. Griffin and Cantrell began wondering what Musk could possibly be doing now, at which point Musk wheeled around and showed them a spreadsheet he'd created. "Hey, guys," he said, "I think we can build this rocket ourselves."

Griffin and Cantrell were too disappointed to even think about Musk's idea at first. They knew all too well the stories of millionaires who thought they could conquer space only to lose their fortunes. But Elon said, "No, I'm serious. I have this spreadsheet." Musk passed his laptop over to Griffin and Cantrell, and they were dumbfounded. The document detailed the costs of the materials needed to build, assemble, and launch a rocket.

According to Musk's calculations, he could undercut existing launch companies by building a smaller rocket that would focus on carrying smaller satellites and research equipment to space. The spreadsheet also laid out the hypothetical performance characteristics of the rocket—information on how much it would weigh, how fast it would go, what type of fuel it would need—in fairly impressive detail. "I said, 'Elon, where did you get this?'" Cantrell said.

Musk had spent months studying the aerospace industry and the physics behind it. From Cantrell and others, he'd borrowed *Rocket Propulsion Elements* and *Fundamentals of Astrodynamics*, along with several more important texts. Musk had reverted to his childhood state as a devourer of information and had realized that rockets could and should be made much cheaper than what the Russians were offering. Forget the mice. Forget the plant with its own video feed growing—or possibly dying—on Mars. Musk would inspire people to think about exploring space again by making it cheaper to explore space.

8

SPACEX TAKES FLIGHT . . . SORT OF

WHEN ELON FIRST TOYED WITH the idea of entering the space business on his flight home from Moscow in February 2002, he could have named several businessmen who had committed many millions to making a go of building rockets commercially—only to fail miserably. Musk had at least one reason to think he might be the first to succeed where so many others had not. That reason's name was Tom Mueller.

Mueller had been tinkering with and building rockets since he was kid. He started by putting together rockets from mail-order kits but rather quickly graduated to designing and making his own. After college, he got jobs working on satellites, propellants, and engines at big aerospace companies like TRW, and he also continued building rockets as a hobby.

In January 2002, Mueller was hanging out in the workshop of a friend, fiddling around with an eighty-pound engine, when Elon stopped by. Cantrell had recommended that Musk check out the workshop and see Mueller's designs. Mueller had the eighty-pound engine on his shoulder and was trying to bolt it to a support structure when Musk began asking him questions. "He asked me how much thrust it had," Mueller said. "He wanted to know if I had ever worked on anything bigger. I told him that, yeah, I'd worked on a 650,000-pound thrust engine at TRW and knew every part of it." Mueller set the engine down and tried to keep up with Musk's interrogation. "How much would that big engine cost?" Musk asked. Mueller told him TRW built it for about $12 million. Musk shot back, "Yeah, but how much could you really do it for?"

Mueller ended up talking with Musk for hours. The next weekend, Mueller invited Musk to his house to continue their discussion. Musk knew he had found someone who really knew the ins and outs of making rockets. After that, Musk introduced Mueller to the rest of his team of space experts. Mueller was impressed by all of them.

He helped Musk fill out that spreadsheet about the cost of a new rocket. The rocket would not carry truck-size satellites like some of the monster rockets flown by Boeing,

Lockheed, and Russia and other countries. Instead, the rocket was based on the idea that a whole new group of people and companies might want to send smaller loads for research and experimentation to space if a company could drastically lower the price per launch. Musk loved the idea of developing the workhorse of a new era in space.

Of course, all of this was just talk—and then, suddenly, it wasn't. PayPal had gone public in February 2002 with its shares shooting up 55 percent, and Musk knew that eBay wanted to buy the company as well. While he thought about the rocket idea, Musk's net worth had increased from tens of millions to hundreds of millions. In April 2002, Musk fully abandoned the publicity-stunt idea and committed to building a proper space company. He pulled aside Cantrell, Griffin, Mueller, and Chris Thompson, an aerospace engineer at Boeing, and told the group, "I want to do this company. If you guys are in, let's do it."

Founded in June 2002, Space Exploration Technologies (SpaceX) came to life in humble settings. Musk acquired an old warehouse in El Segundo, a suburb of Los Angeles filled with aerospace companies. During the first week of SpaceX's operations, delivery trucks showed up packed full of Dell laptops and printers and folding tables that would serve as the first desks. Musk walked over to one of the loading docks, rolled up the door, and offloaded the equipment himself.

Musk had soon transformed the SpaceX office with a fresh coat of white paint slathered onto the walls. Desks were interspersed around the factory so that Ivy League computer scientists and engineers designing the machines could sit with the welders and machinists building the hardware. This approach stood as SpaceX's first major break with traditional aerospace companies that prefer to separate different engineering groups from one another and from machinists.

As the first dozen or so employees came to the offices, they were told that SpaceX would build its own engines and then work with suppliers for the other components of the rocket. The company would gain an edge over the competition by building a better, cheaper engine and by improving the assembly process to make rockets faster and cheaper than anyone else. This vision included the construction of a type of mobile launch vehicle that could travel to various sites, take the rocket from a horizontal to vertical position, and send it off to space—no muss, no fuss. SpaceX was meant to get so good at this process that it could do multiple launches a month and make money off each one.

SpaceX was to be America's attempt at a redo in the rocket business. Musk felt that the space industry had not really improved in about fifty years. The aerospace companies had little competition and tended to make very expensive products that achieved maximum performance, even when something less expensive and less powerful would do just as well.

SpaceX built its rocket factory from the ground up in a Los Angeles warehouse to give birth to the Falcon 1 rocket. Photograph courtesy of SpaceX

Musk declared that SpaceX's first rocket would be called the Falcon 1, a nod to Star Wars's Millennium Falcon. At a time when the cost of sending a 550-pound load started at $30 million, he promised that the Falcon 1 would be able to carry a 1,400-pound load for $6.9 million.

As space enthusiasts started to learn about the new company, they were thrilled that someone had decided to take the cheap and fast approach. Some members of the military had already been promoting the idea of giving the armed forces more aggressive space capabilities for what they called "responsive space." If a conflict broke out, the military wanted the ability to respond with satellites built uniquely for that mission. This would mean moving away from a model where it takes ten years to build and deploy a satellite for a specific job. Instead, the military desired cheaper, smaller satellites that could be changed through software and sent up on short notice, almost like disposable satellites.

Like the military, scientists wanted cheap, quick access to space and the ability to send up experiments and get data back on a regular basis. Some companies in other industries were also interested in rides to space to study how a lack of gravity affected the properties of their products.

As good as a cheap launch vehicle sounded, the odds of a private citizen building one that worked were beyond remote. The rockets used to transport things to space are mostly modified missiles developed through decades of trial and error and paid for by billions upon billions of government dollars. SpaceX did not have a budget that could support a string of explosions as it learned the rocket-building craft. At best, SpaceX would have three or four shots at making the Falcon 1 work. "People thought we were just crazy," Mueller said. "At TRW, I had an army of people and government funding. Now we were going to make a low-cost rocket from scratch with a small team. People just didn't think it could be done."

Gripped by the excitement of this daring enterprise, Musk threw more than $100 million of his PayPal money at SpaceX in July of 2002. With such a massive up-front investment, no one would be able to wrestle control of SpaceX away from Musk as they had done at Zip2 and PayPal.

And then all of a sudden none of this seemed to matter. Justine had given birth to a son—Nevada Alexander Musk. He was ten weeks old when, just as the eBay deal was announced, he died. The Musks had tucked Nevada in for a nap and placed the boy on his back as parents are taught to do. When they returned to check on him, he was no longer breathing.

Following Nevada's death, Musk was devastated but stoic, refusing to express much emotion. "It made me extremely sad to talk about it," Musk said. "I'm not sure why I'd want to talk about extremely sad events. It does no good for the future. If you've got other kids and obligations, then wallowing in sadness does no good for anyone around you. I'm not sure what should be done in such situations."

He decided to try and think about something else by throwing himself into the work at SpaceX and rapidly expanded the company's goals. His conversations with aerospace suppliers left Musk frustrated. It sounded like they all charged a lot of money and worked slowly. The plan to stitch together parts made by these types of companies gave way to the decision to make as much as practical right at SpaceX.

Musk hired an all-star crew as the SpaceX top executives, including Mueller. Mueller set to work right away building two engines—Merlin and Kestrel, named after two types of falcons. Musk also recruited Gwynne Shotwell, an aerospace veteran who started as SpaceX's first salesperson and rose in the years that followed to be president and Musk's right-hand woman.

Tom Mueller (far right, gray shirt) led the design, testing, and construction of SpaceX's engines. Photograph courtesy of SpaceX

These early days marked the arrival of Mary Beth Brown as well. Brown—or MB, as everyone called her— became Musk's loyal assistant, establishing a real-life version of the relationship between *Iron Man*'s Tony Stark and Pepper Potts. If Musk worked a twenty-hour day, so did Brown. Over the years, she brought Musk meals, set up his business appointments, arranged time with his children, picked out his clothes, dealt with press requests, and, when necessary, yanked Musk out of meetings to keep him on schedule. She became the only bridge between Musk and all of his companies.

Brown's greatest gift, though, may have been reading Musk's moods. At both SpaceX and Tesla, Brown placed her desk a few feet in front of Musk's so that people had to pass her before having a meeting with him. If someone needed to request permission to buy an expensive item, they would stop for a moment in front of Brown and wait for a nod to go see Musk or the shake to go away because Musk was having a bad day.

The rank-and-file engineers at SpaceX tended to be young male overachievers. Musk would personally reach out to the aerospace departments of top colleges and inquire about the students who had finished with the best marks on their exams. It was not unusual for him to call the students in their dorm rooms and recruit them over the phone.

"I thought it was a prank call," said Michael Colonno, who heard from Musk while attending Stanford. "I did not believe for a minute that he had a rocket company." Once the students looked Musk up on the internet, selling them on SpaceX was easy. For the first time in years if not decades, young aeronautics whizzes who wanted to explore space had a really exciting company they could work for, and maybe design a rocket, or possibly, become an astronaut. As word of SpaceX's ambitions spread, top engineers from Boeing, Lockheed Martin, and Orbital Sciences fled to the upstart too.

The SpaceX engineers talked Musk into buying a three-hundred-acre test site in McGregor, Texas, a small city near the center of the state. The navy had tested rockets on the land years before and so too had Andrew Beal, a banking billionaire, before his aerospace company collapsed. Both the navy and Beal had left behind a lot of very useful infrastructure.

Jeremy Hollman was one of the young engineers who soon found himself living in Texas and customizing the test site to SpaceX's needs. Hollman was exactly the kind of recruit Musk wanted: he'd earned an aerospace engineering degree and a masters in astronautical engineering, and he'd spent a couple of years working as a test engineer at Boeing dealing with jets, rockets, and spacecraft.

SpaceX tests new engines and crafts at a site in McGregor, Texas. Here the company is testing a reusable rocket, code-named "Grasshopper," that can land itself. Photograph courtesy of SpaceX

To Hollman, every project at Boeing felt large, cumbersome, and costly. So when Musk came along selling radical change, Hollman jumped. "I thought it was an opportunity I could not pass up," he said. At twenty-three, Hollman was young, single, and willing to give up any social life in favor of working at SpaceX nonstop. He became Mueller's second in command.

Mueller had developed a pair of three-dimensional computer models of the two engines he wanted to build. Merlin would be the engine for the first stage of the Falcon 1, which lifted it off the ground, and Kestrel would be the smaller engine used to power the upper, second stage of the rocket and guide it in space to drop off a satellite or other payload, like scientific equipment and supplies for the space station. Together, Hollman and Mueller figured out which parts of the engines SpaceX would build at the factory and which parts it would try to buy. During this process, Hollman found that creativity got him a long way. He discovered, for example, that changing the seals on some readily available car wash valves made them good enough to be used with rocket fuel and helped SpaceX avoid wasting money on more costly, specialized valves.

After SpaceX completed its first engine at the factory in California, Hollman loaded it and lots of other equipment into a trailer. He then drove four thousand pounds of gear from Los Angeles to Texas and the test site. Amid rattlesnakes, fire ants, and searing heat, the group, led by Tim Buzza, a former Boeing engineer, and Mueller began the process of exploring every detail of the engines.

From that point on, the trek from California to the test site became known as the Texas Cattle Haul. The SpaceX engineers would work for ten days straight, come back to California for a weekend, and then head back. To ease the burden of travel, Musk sometimes let them use his private jet. "It carried six people," Mueller said. "Well, seven if someone sat on the toilet, which happened all the time."

The locals in town rarely complained about the noise

of the test engines, although the animals on nearby farms seemed less impressed. "Cows have this natural defense mechanism where they gather and start running in a circle," Hollman said. "Every time we fired an engine, the cows scattered and then got in that circle with the younger ones placed in the middle. We set up a cow cam to watch them."

Both Kestrel and Merlin came with challenges, and they were treated as alternating engineering exercises. "We would run Merlin until we ran out of hardware or did something bad," Mueller said. "Then we'd run Kestrel, and there was never a shortage of things to do." For months, the SpaceX engineers arrived at the site at eight a.m. and spent twelve hours there working on the engines before going to Outback Steakhouse for dinner. Mueller would look over the test data and spot some problem. He would call California and prescribe hardware changes. The engineers would change the parts and send them off to Texas. Often the workers in Texas modified parts themselves using equipment that Mueller had brought out to their workshop.

Some members of the Texas crew perfected their skills to the point that they could build a test-worthy engine in three days. "There was an almost addictive quality to the experience," Hollman said. "You're twenty-four or twenty-five, and they're trusting you with so much. It was very empowering."

To get to space, the Merlin engine would need to burn for

180 seconds. That seemed like an eternity for the engineers when they first arrived in Texas. Then, the engine would burn for only a half second before it died. Sometimes Merlin vibrated too much during the tests. Sometimes it responded badly to a new material. Sometimes it cracked and needed major part upgrades.

Musk would not tolerate excuses or the lack of a clear plan to fix problems. Hollman was one of many engineers who arrived at this realization after facing one of Musk's interrogations. "The worst call was the first one," Hollman said. "Something had gone wrong, and Elon asked me how long it would take to be operational again, and I didn't have an immediate answer. He said, 'You need to. This is important to the company. Everything is riding on this. Why don't you have an answer?' He kept hitting me with pointed, direct questions. I thought it was more important to let him know quickly what happened, but I learned it was more important to have all the information."

Even as it struggled to work through the issues with its engines, SpaceX managed to pick up its first customers in 2003. The company declared that its initial rocket would launch in "early 2004" from Vandenberg Air Force Base in California, carrying a satellite for the Department of Defense. With this goal looming, twelve-hour days, six days a week were considered the norm, although many people worked longer than that for extended periods of time.

Breaks, as far they existed, came around eight p.m. on some weeknights back at SpaceX's headquarters in El Segundo when Musk would allow everyone to use their work computers to play first-person-shooter video games like Quake III Arena and Counter-Strike against one another. The sound of guns loading could be heard throughout the office as close to twenty people armed themselves for battle. Musk often won the games. "The CEO is there shooting at us with rockets and plasma guns," said Colonno. "Worse, he's almost alarmingly good at these games and has insanely fast reactions. He knew all the tricks and how to sneak up on people."

These gaming sessions were a welcome relief with the pressure mounting for SpaceX employees. Before it had even flown its first rocket, SpaceX revealed plans to start work on a second, larger rocket. Along with the Falcon 1, it would build the Falcon 5. Per the name, this rocket would have five engines and could carry more weight—9,200 pounds—to low orbit around Earth. The Falcon 5 would also be designed to reach the International Space Station for resupply missions— a capability that would open up SpaceX for some large NASA contracts. And the rocket would come with unprecedented safety and reliability features like the ability to complete its missions even if three of the five engines failed.

In order to keep up with all this work, SpaceX and Musk set out to hire the best talent. As the new hires arrived, SpaceX moved beyond its original building to fill up several buildings in the same El Segundo complex.

The engineers were running sophisticated software and dealing with large files, so they needed high-speed connections between all of these offices. But SpaceX had neighbors who were blocking a plan to connect all of its buildings through fiber-optic lines. Instead of taking the time to haggle with the other companies, the IT chief, Branden Spikes, who had worked with Musk at Zip2 and PayPal, came up with a quicker, more devious solution.

A friend of his worked for the phone company and drew a diagram that demonstrated a way to squeeze a networking cable safely between the electricity, cable, and phone wires on a telephone pole. At two a.m., an off-the-books crew showed up with a cherry picker and ran fiber to the telephone poles and then cables straight to the SpaceX buildings. "We did that over a weekend instead of taking months to get permits," Spikes said. "There was always this feeling that we were facing a sort of insurmountable challenge and that we had to band together to fight the good fight."

The early part of 2004, when SpaceX had once hoped to launch its first rocket, came and went. The Merlin engine that Mueller and his team had built appeared to be among the most efficient rocket engines ever made. It was just taking longer than Musk had expected to pass tests needed to clear the engine for a launch. But, by the fall of 2004, the engines were burning consistently and meeting all their requirements.

This meant that Mueller and his team could breathe easy and that everyone else at SpaceX should prepare to suffer. Mueller had spent SpaceX's entire existence as the "critical path"—the person holding up the company from achieving its next steps—working under Musk's close inspection. "With the engine ready, it was time for mass panic," Mueller said. "No one else knew what it was like to be on critical path."

With the engines in working order, the rest of the rocket needed to be perfected and put together. In May of 2005, SpaceX managed to pull everything together and transported a fully functional rocket 180 miles north to Vandenberg Air Force Base for a test fire. It completed a five-second burn on the launchpad.

Continuing to launch from Vandenberg would have been very convenient for SpaceX. The site is close to Los Angeles and has several launchpads to pick from. SpaceX, though, became an unwelcome guest. Lockheed and Boeing, which fly billion-dollar spy satellites to space for the military from Vandenberg, didn't like SpaceX's presence—in part because SpaceX represented a threat to their business, and in part because this unpredictable start-up was mucking around near their precious cargo. As SpaceX started to move from the testing phase to the launch phase, it was told it would have to wait months for its turn to use the pads. "Even though they said we could fly, it was clear that we would not," said Gwynne Shotwell.

Gwynne Shotwell is Musk's right-hand woman at SpaceX, and oversees the day-to-day operations of the company, including monitoring a launch from mission control. Photograph courtesy of SpaceX

Searching for a new launch site, Shotwell and aerospace engineer Hans Koenigsmann put a projection of the world up on the wall and looked for a place along the equator. At the equator, the planet spins faster and gives rockets an added boost. The location also makes it easier to put satellites into equatorial orbits. The first name that jumped out was Kwajalein Island—or Kwaj—the largest island in an atoll between Guam and Hawaii in the Pacific Ocean and part of the Republic of the Marshall Islands. About one hundred islands make up the Kwajalein Atoll. Many of them stretch for just a few hundred yards and are much longer than they are wide. Shotwell recognized Kwajalein Island because the US Army had used it for decades as a missile test site.

Shotwell looked up the name of a colonel at the test site and sent him an email. Three weeks later, she got a call back with the army saying they would love to have SpaceX fly from the islands. In June 2005, SpaceX's engineers began to fill containers with their equipment to ship them to Kwaj.

To get to Kwaj, the SpaceX employees either flew on Musk's jet or took commercial flights through Hawaii. In the beginning, the SpaceX workers stayed in two-bedroom suites on Kwajalein Island that looked more like dormitories than hotel rooms. Any materials that the engineers needed had to be flown in on Musk's plane or were more often brought by boat from Hawaii or the mainland United States. Each day, the SpaceX crew gathered their gear and took a forty-five-minute boat ride to Omelek, a seven-acre, palm-tree-and-vegetation-covered island that would be transformed into their launchpad.

Over the course of several months, a small team of people cleared the brush, poured concrete to support the launchpad, and converted a double-wide trailer into offices.

The work was exhausting and took place in soul-sapping humidity under a sun powerful enough to burn the skin through a T-shirt. Eventually, some of the workers preferred to spend the night on Omelek rather than making the journey through rough waters back to the main island. "Some of the offices were turned into bedrooms with mattresses and cots," Hollman said. "Then we shipped over a very nice refrigerator and a good grill and plumbed in a shower. We tried to make it less like camping and more like living."

The sun rose at seven a.m. each day, and that's when the SpaceX team got to work. As the large structures arrived, the workers placed the body of the rocket horizontally in a makeshift hangar and spent hours melding together all of its parts. "There was always something to do," Hollman said. "If the engine wasn't a problem, then there was an avionics problem or a software problem."

The workers wanted to pave a two-hundred-yard pathway between the hangar and the launchpad to make it easier to transport the rocket. Musk refused. This left the engineers moving the rocket and its wheeled support structures in the fashion of ancient Egyptians. They laid down a series of wooden planks and rolled the rocket across them, grabbing the last piece of wood from the back and running it forward in a continuous cycle.

By seven p.m. each day, the engineers finished up their

work. "One or two people would decide it was their night to cook, and they would make steak and potatoes and pasta," Hollman said. "We had a bunch of movies and a DVD player, and some of us did a lot of fishing off the docks." For many of the engineers, this was both a torturous and magical experience. "Every person on that island was a ... star, and they were always holding seminars on radios or the engine. It was such an invigorating place," said Walter Sims, a SpaceX tech expert.

SpaceX had to conduct its first flights from Kwajalein Atoll (or Kwaj) in the Marshall Islands. The island experience was a difficult but ultimately fruitful adventure for the engineers. Photograph courtesy of SpaceX

Finally, on March 24, 2006, after a few failed launch attempts, it was all systems go. The Falcon 1 stood on its square launchpad and ignited. It soared into the sky, turning the island below it into a green speck amid a vast blue expanse. In the control room, Musk paced as he watched the action. Then, about twenty-five seconds in, it became clear that all was not well. A fire broke out above the Merlin engine, and suddenly this machine, which had been flying straight and true, started to spin and then tumble uncontrollably back to earth. The Falcon 1 ended up falling directly down onto the launch site. Most of the wreck fell into a reef 250 feet from the launchpad, and the satellite cargo smashed through SpaceX's machine shop roof and landed more or less intact on the floor. Some of the engineers put on their snorkeling and scuba gear and recovered the pieces.

Musk and other SpaceX executives blamed the crash on an unnamed technician. They said this technician had done some work on the rocket one day before the launch and failed to properly tighten a fitting on a fuel pipe, which caused the fitting to crack. The fitting in question was something basic—an aluminum b-nut that's often used to connect a pair of tubes. The technician was Hollman. In the aftermath of the rocket crash, Hollman flew to Los Angeles to confront Musk directly. He'd spent years working day and night on the Falcon 1 and felt enraged that Musk had called out him and his team in public. Hollman knew that he'd fastened the b-nut correctly and that observers from NASA had been looking over his shoulder to check the work. When Hollman charged into SpaceX's headquarters with a head full of fury, Brown tried to calm him and stop him from seeing Musk. Hollman kept going anyway, and the two of them proceeded to have a shouting match at Musk's cubicle.

After all the rubbish was analyzed, it turned out that the b-nut had almost certainly cracked due to corrosion from the months in Kwaj's salty atmosphere. "The rocket was literally crusted with salt on one side, and you had to scrape it off," Mueller said. "But we had done a static fire three days earlier, and everything was fine." SpaceX had tried to save about fifty pounds of weight by using aluminum components instead of stainless steel. Years later, a number of SpaceX's executives still agonize over the way Hollman and his team were treated. "They were our best guys, and they kind of got blamed to get an answer out to the world," Mueller said. "That was really bad. We found out later that it was dumb luck."

After the crash, Musk wanted to launch again within six months, but putting together a new machine would require an immense amount of work. SpaceX had some pieces for a second rocket ready in El Segundo but certainly not a whole ready-to-fire rocket.

Ultimately, it took about a year to prepare the rocket for another launch. The engineers had been careful with their work, vowing to be more disciplined and to function better as a cohesive group. On March 21, 2007, the Falcon 1 surged up out of the palm trees and toward space. It flew for a couple of minutes with engineers now and again reporting that the systems were "nominal," or in good shape. At three minutes into the flight, the first stage of the rocket separated and fell back to Earth, and the Kestrel engine kicked in as planned to carry the second stage into orbit. Ecstatic cheers went out in the control room. Next, at the four-minute mark, the fairing—a type of case that holds the payload—atop the rocket separated as planned.

"It was doing exactly what it was supposed to do," said Mueller. "I was sitting next to Elon and looked at him and said, 'We've made it.' We're hugging and believe it's going to make it to orbit. Then it starts to wiggle." For more than five glorious minutes, the SpaceX engineers got to feel like they had done everything right. But then that wiggle that Mueller noticed turned into flailing, and the machine swooned, started to break apart, and blew up.

This time the SpaceX engineers were quick to figure out what went wrong. As the propellant was consumed, what was left started to move around the tank and slosh against the sides. The sloshing propellant triggered the wobbling, and at one point it sloshed enough to leave an opening to the engine exposed. When the engine sucked in a big breath of air, it flamed out.

The failure was another crushing blow to SpaceX's engineers. Some of them had spent close to two years shuffling back and forth among California, Hawaii, and Kwaj. By the time SpaceX could attempt another launch, it would be about four years after Musk's original target, and the company had been chewing through his internet fortune at a worrying rate. Musk had vowed publicly that he would see this thing through to the end, but people inside and outside the company were doing the math and could tell that SpaceX likely could only afford one more attempt—maybe two. To survive, SpaceX needed a successful launch.

9

ALL ELECTRIC

JB STRAUBEL HAS A TWO-INCH-LONG scar that cuts across the middle of his left cheek. He earned it in high school during a chemistry class experiment. Straubel whipped up the wrong mix of chemicals, and the beaker he was holding exploded, throwing off shards of glass, one of which sliced through his face.

The wound lingers as a tinkerer's badge of honor. It arrived near the end of a childhood full of experimentation with chemicals and machines. Born in Wisconsin, Straubel constructed a large chemistry lab in the basement of his family's home that included fume hoods and chemicals ordered, borrowed, or stolen. At thirteen, Straubel found an old golf cart at the dump. He brought it back home and restored it to working condition, which required him to rebuild the electric motor.

It seemed that Straubel was always taking something apart, sprucing it up, and putting it back together. Straubel's inquisitive spirit carried him west to Stanford University, where he enrolled in 1994 intending to become a physicist. After flying through the hardest courses he could take, Straubel concluded that majoring in physics would not be for him. The advanced courses were too theoretical, and Straubel liked to get his hands dirty. He developed his own major, called "energy systems and engineering." "I wanted to take software and electricity and use it to control energy," Straubel said. "It was computing combined with power electronics. I collected all the things I love doing in one place."

There was no major clean-technology movement at this time, but there were companies dabbling with new uses for solar power and electric vehicles. Straubel ended up hunting down these start-ups, hanging out in their garages, and pestering the engineers. He began tinkering once again on his own as well in the garage of a house he shared with a half dozen friends. Straubel bought a used, beat-up Porsche for $1,600 and turned it into an electric car. The car set the world record for electric vehicle (EV) acceleration, traveling a quarter mile in 17.28 seconds. "The thing

I took away was that the electronics were great, and you could get acceleration on a shoestring budget, but the batteries sucked," Straubel said. "It had a thirty-mile range, so I learned firsthand about some of the limitations of electric vehicles." Straubel gave his car a hybrid boost, building a gasoline-powered contraption that could be towed behind the Porsche and used to recharge the batteries. It was good enough for Straubel to drive the four hundred miles down to Los Angeles and back.

By 2002, Straubel was living in Los Angeles. He'd gotten a masters degree from Stanford and bounced around a couple of companies looking for something that called out to him. He decided on Rosen Motors, which had built one of the world's first hybrid vehicles. After it folded, Straubel followed Harold Rosen, a famed engineer, to create an electric plane. "I'm a pilot and love to fly, so this was perfect for me," Straubel said. To help make ends meet, Straubel also worked nights and on the weekends doing electronics consulting for a start-up.

It was in the midst of toiling away on all these projects that some of Straubel's old buddies from the Stanford solar car team came to pay him a visit. Groups of rogue engineers at Stanford had been working on solar cars for years. Unlike today, when the university would jump at the chance to support such a project, Stanford tried to shut down this group of fringe freaks and geeks. The students proved very capable of doing the work on their own and competed in cross-country solar-powered car races.

JB Straubel puts together one of Tesla Motors's early battery packs at his house. Photograph courtesy of Tesla Motors

Straubel helped build the vehicles during his time at university and even after, forming relationships with the incoming crop of engineers. The team had just raced 2,300 miles from Chicago to Los Angeles, and Straubel offered the broke, exhausted kids a place to stay. About a half dozen students showed up at Straubel's place, took their first showers in many days, and then spread across his floor. As they chatted late into the night, Straubel and the solar team kept coming back to one topic. They realized that lithium ion batteries—such as the ones in their car being fed by the sun—had gotten much better than most people realized. Many consumer electronics devices like laptops were running on so-called 18650 lithium ion batteries, which looked a lot like AA batteries and could be strung together. "We wondered what would happen if you put ten thousand of the battery cells together," Straubel said. "We did the math and figured you could go almost one thousand miles. It was totally nerdy . . . and eventually everyone fell asleep, but the idea really stuck with me."

Soon enough, Straubel was stalking the solar car crew, trying to talk them into building an electric car based on the lithium ion batteries. The Stanford students agreed to join Straubel, if he could raise some money. He began going to trade shows handing out brochures about his idea and emailing just about anyone he could think of. "I was shameless," he said. The only problem was that no one had any interest in what Straubel was selling. Investors dealt him one rejection after another for months on end. Then, in the fall of 2003, Straubel met Elon Musk.

Harold Rosen had set up a lunch with Musk at a seafood restaurant near the SpaceX headquarters in Los Angeles and brought Straubel along to help talk up the electric plane idea. When Musk wasn't interested in planes, Straubel announced his electric car side project. The crazy idea struck an immediate chord with Musk, who had been thinking about electric vehicles for years. While Musk had mostly focused on using ultracapacitors for the vehicles, he was thrilled and surprised to hear how far the lithium ion battery technology had progressed. "Everyone else had told me I was nuts, but Elon loved the idea," Straubel said. "He said, 'Sure, I will give you some money.'" Musk promised Straubel $10,000 of the $100,000 he was seeking. On the spot, Musk and Straubel formed a kinship that would survive more than a decade of extreme highs and lows as they set out to do nothing less than change the world.

After the meeting with Musk, Straubel reached out to his friends at AC Propulsion. The Los Angeles–based company built everything from zippy midsize passenger cars right on up to sports cars. Straubel really wanted to show Musk the tzero (from "T-minus zero")—the highest-end vehicle that AC Propulsion's made. It was a type of kit car that had a fiberglass body sitting on top of a steel frame and went from zero to sixty miles per hour in 4.9 seconds when first unveiled in 1997.

Straubel had spent years hanging out with the AC Propulsion crew and asked Tom Gage, the company's president, to bring a tzero over for Musk to drive. Musk fell for the car. He saw its potential as a screaming-fast machine that could shift the perception of electric cars from being slow and boring to being something aspirational. For months Musk offered to fund an effort to transform the kit car into a commercial vehicle but was turned down time and again. "It was a proof of concept and needed to be made real," Straubel said. "I love . . . the AC Propulsion guys, but they were sort of hopeless at business and refused to do it." While the meetings with AC Propulsion didn't result in a deal, they had solidified Musk's interest in backing something well beyond Straubel's science project.

Unbeknownst to Straubel, at about the same time, a couple of business partners in Northern California had also fallen in love with the idea of making a lithium ion battery–powered car. Martin Eberhard and Marc Tarpenning had founded NuvoMedia in 1997 to create one of the earliest electronic book readers, called the Rocket eBook. The work at NuvoMedia had given the men insight into the hugely improved lithium ion batteries used to power laptops and other portable devices. While the Rocket eBook was too far ahead of its time and not a major commercial success, it was innovative enough that a company called Gemstar International Group purchased NuvoMedia in March 2000 for $187 million.

Spoils in hand, the cofounders stayed in touch after the

deal. They both lived in Woodside, one of the wealthiest towns in Silicon Valley, and chatted from time to time about what they should tackle next. "We thought up some goofball things," said Tarpenning. "But nothing really resonated, and we wanted something more important."

Eberhard was a supremely talented engineer with a do-gooder's social conscience. The United States's repeated conflicts in the Middle East and squabbles over oil bothered him, and like many other science-minded folks around 2000 he had started to accept global warming as a reality. Eberhard began looking for alternatives to gas-guzzling cars. Eberhard also became interested in the all-electric cars from AC Propulsion. He too urged AC Propulsion to become a commercial enterprise rather than a hobby shop. When they rejected him, Eberhard decided to form his own company and see what the lithium ion batteries could really do.

Eberhard began with building a technical model of the electric car on a spreadsheet. This let him tweak various components and see how they might affect the vehicle's shape and performance. He could adjust the weight, number of batteries, and resistance of the tires and body, and then get back answers on how many batteries it would take to power the various designs. The models made it clear that the technology seemed to favor a lighter-weight, high-end sports car, which would be fast, fun to drive, and have far better range than most people would expect.

Eberhard and Tarpenning figured they could build something for the $3 billion-per-year luxury auto market in the United States that would let rich people have fun and feel good about themselves too. "People pay for cool and sexy and an amazing zero-to-sixty time," Tarpenning said.

On July 1, 2003, Eberhard and Tarpenning formed their new company. A few months earlier, Eberhard had come up with the name Tesla Motors, both to honor electric motor pioneer Nikola Tesla and because it sounded cool. The cofounders rented an office that had three desks and two small rooms in Menlo Park, California. The third desk was occupied a few months later by Ian Wright, an engineer who grew up on a farm in New Zealand. As the three men began to tell some of their confidants of their plans, people thought they were joking.

Anyone who tries to build a car company in the United States is quickly reminded that the last successful start-up in the industry was Chrysler, founded in 1925. Designing and building a car from the ground up comes with plenty of challenges, but it's really getting the money and know-how to build lots of cars that has stopped past efforts to get a new company going.

The Tesla founders were aware of these realities. They

figured that Nikola Tesla had built an electric motor a century earlier, so that was feasible. They also felt capable enough to create a drivetrain, or the collection of parts needed, to take the power from the motor and send it to the wheels. The frightening part of their enterprise would be building the factory to make the car and all its parts.

The plan the Tesla cofounders came up with was to purchase some technology from AC Propulsion around the tzero vehicle and to use the Lotus Elise chassis for the body of their car. Lotus, an English carmaker, had released the two-door Elise in 1996, and its sleek, ground-hugging style appealed to wealthy car buyers. After talking to a number of people in the car dealership business, the Tesla team decided to avoid selling their cars through partners and sell directly. With these basics of a plan in place, the three men went hunting for some funds from investors in January 2004.

No investors were interested, however, with the exception of two companies, and even they didn't sound excited. The lead partner at one of them had made a lot of money on NuvoMedia and felt some loyalty to Eberhard and Tarpenning. "He said, 'This is stupid, but I have invested in every automotive start-up for the last forty years, so why not?'" Tarpenning recalled. Tesla still needed a lead investor who would give them the bulk of the $7 million needed to make what's known as a mule or a prototype vehicle. That would be their first milestone and give them something physical to show off, which could aid a second round of funding.

Eberhard and Tarpenning had Elon Musk's name in the back of their heads as a possible lead investor from the beginning. They had both seen him speak a couple of years earlier at a Mars Society conference held at Stanford where Musk had laid out his vision of sending mice into space, and they got the impression that he thought a bit differently and would be open to the idea of an electric car.

Eberhard and Wright flew down to Los Angeles and met with Musk on a Friday. That weekend, Musk peppered Tarpenning, who had been away on a trip, with questions about the financial model. "I just remember responding, responding, and responding," Tarpenning said. "The following Monday, Martin and I flew down to meet him again, and he said, 'Okay, I'm in.'"

The Tesla founders felt like they had lucked into the perfect investor. Musk had the engineering smarts to know what they were building. He also shared their larger goal of trying to end the United States's addiction to oil. "You need angel investors to have some belief, and it wasn't a purely financial transaction for him," Tarpenning said. "He wanted to change the energy equation of the country." The $6.5 million investment in Tesla made Musk its largest shareholder.

Not long after this meeting took place, Musk called Straubel and urged him to meet with the Tesla team. Straubel heard that their offices in Menlo Park were about a half mile from his house. He was intrigued but very skeptical of their story. No one on the planet was more dialed in to the electric vehicle scene than Straubel, and he found it hard to believe that a couple of guys had gotten this far along without word of their project reaching him. Nonetheless, Straubel stopped by the office for a meeting and was hired right away in May 2004. "I told them that I had been building the battery pack they need down the street with funding from Elon," Straubel said. "We agreed to join forces and formed this ragtag group."

10

SILICON VALLEY LEARNS TO DRIVE

HAD ANYONE FROM DETROIT—THE TRADITIONAL car capital of the US—stopped by Tesla Motors at this point, they would have laughed out loud. The sum total of the company's automotive expertise was that a couple of the guys at Tesla really liked cars and another one had created a series of science fair projects based on technology that the automotive industry considered ridiculous. What's more, the founding team had no intention of turning to Detroit for advice on how to build a car company. No, Tesla would do what every other Silicon Valley start-up had done before it, which was hire a bunch of young, hungry engineers and figure things out as they went along. Never mind that the Bay Area had no real history of this model ever having worked for something like a car, and that building a complex physical object had little in common with writing a software application. What Tesla did have, ahead of anyone else, was the realization that 18650 lithium ion batteries had gotten really good and were going to keep getting better. Hopefully that coupled with some effort and smarts would be enough.

Straubel had a direct pipeline into the smart, energetic engineers at Stanford and told many of them about Tesla. Gene Berdichevsky, one of the members of the solar-powered-car team, lit up the second he heard from Straubel. An undergraduate, Berdichevsky volunteered to quit school, work for free, and sweep the floors at Tesla if that's what it took to get a job. The founders were impressed with his spirit and hired Berdichevsky after one meeting. This left Berdichevsky in the uncomfortable position of calling his Russian immigrant parents, a pair of nuclear submarine engineers, to tell them that he was giving up on Stanford to join an electric car start-up. As employee number seven, he spent part of the workday in the Menlo Park office and the rest in Straubel's living room. He was designing three-dimensional models of the car's powertrain—the series of parts that delivers power from the motor to the wheels—on a computer and building battery pack prototypes in the garage. "Only now do I realize how insane it was," Berdichevsky said.

Tesla soon needed to expand to accommodate its budding engineer army and to create a workshop that would help bring the Roadster, as they were now calling the car, to life. They found a two-story industrial building in San Carlos, California. The ten-thousand-square-foot facility wasn't much, but it had room to build a research and development (R&D) shop capable of knocking out some prototype cars.

Berdichevsky painted the office white on a Sunday night, and the next week the employees made a field trip to IKEA to buy desks and hopped online to order their computers from Dell. As for tools, Tesla had a single Craftsman toolbox loaded with hammers, nails, and other carpentry basics. Musk would visit now and again from Los Angeles and was unfazed by the conditions, having seen SpaceX grow up in similar surroundings.

The original plan for producing a prototype vehicle sounded simple. Tesla would take the AC Propulsion tzero powertrain and fit it into the Lotus Elise body. The company had acquired a diagram for an electric motor design and figured it could buy a transmission from a company in the United States or Europe and outsource any other parts from Asia. Tesla's engineers mostly needed to focus on developing the battery pack systems, wiring the car, and cutting and welding metal as needed to bring everything together. The Tesla team thought of the Roadster as something that could be done with two or three mechanical engineers and a few assembly people.

A handful of engineers built the first Tesla Roadster in a Silicon Valley warehouse that they had turned into a garage workshop and research lab. Photograph courtesy of Tesla Motors

The engineers bought a blue lift for the car and set it up inside the building. They also purchased some machine tools, hand tools, and floodlights to work at night and started to turn the facility into a hotbed of R&D

activity. Electrical engineers studied the Lotus's base-level software to figure out how it tied together the pedals, mechanical apparatus, and the dashboard gauges. The really advanced work took place with the battery pack design. Tesla was groundbreaking in that no one had ever tried to combine hundreds of lithium ion batteries.

The engineers started trying to understand how heat would disperse and current flow would behave across seventy batteries by supergluing them together into groups called "bricks." Then ten bricks would be placed together, and the engineers would test various types of air and liquid cooling mechanisms. When the Tesla team had developed a workable battery pack, they stretched the yellow Lotus Elise chassis five inches and lowered the pack with a crane into the back of the car, where its engine would normally be.

These efforts began in earnest on October 18, 2004, and, rather remarkably, four months later, on January 27, 2005, an entirely new kind of car had been built by eighteen people. It could even be driven around. Tesla had a board meeting that day, and Musk zipped about in the car. He came away happy enough to keep investing. Musk put in $9 million more as Tesla raised $13 million in total in a new round of funding. The company now planned to deliver the Roadster to consumers in early 2006.

Musk and Martin Eberhard prepare to take the early Roadster for a test-drive. Photograph courtesy of Tesla Motors

Once they'd finished building a second car a few months later, the engineers at Tesla decided they needed to face up to a massive potential flaw in their electric vehicle. On July 4, 2005, they were at Eberhard's house in Woodside celebrating Independence Day and figured it was as good a moment as any to see what happened when the Roadster's batteries caught on fire. Someone taped twenty of the batteries together, put a heating strip wire into the bundle, and set it off. "It went up like a cluster of bottle rockets," described David Lyons, a mechanical engineer and employee number twelve. Instead of twenty batteries, the Roadster would have close to seven thousand, and the thought of what an explosion at that scale would be like horrified the engineers.

Tesla formed a six-person task force to deal with the battery issue. They were pulled off all other work and given money to begin running experiments. The first explosions started taking place at the Tesla headquarters, where the engineers filmed them in slow motion. Tesla then moved its explosion research to a blast area behind an electrical substation maintained by the fire department. Blast by blast, the engineers learned a great deal about the inner workings of the batteries. They developed methods for arranging them in ways that would prevent fires from spreading from one battery to the next and other techniques for stopping explosions altogether. Thousands of batteries exploded along the way, and the effort was worth it. It was still early days, for sure, but Tesla was on the verge of inventing battery technology that would set it apart from rivals for years to come. The new technology would become one of the company's great advantages.

The early success at building two prototype cars, coupled with Tesla's engineering breakthroughs around the batteries and other technological pieces, boosted the company's confidence. It was time to put Tesla's stamp on the vehicle. "The original plan had been to do the bare minimum we could get away with as far as making the car stylistically different from a Lotus but electric," said Tarpenning. "Along the way, Elon and the rest of the board said, 'You only get to do this once. It has to delight the customer, and the Lotus just isn't good enough to do that.'"

Musk had a lot of opinions on the design of the body. He wanted a car that Justine could feel comfortable getting into and that had some measure of practicality. Musk made these opinions clear when he visited Tesla for board meetings and design reviews. And so Tesla hired a handful of designers to mock up new looks for the Roadster. After settling on a favorite, the company paid to build a quarter-scale model of the vehicle in January 2005 and then a full-scale model in April.

About a year later, in May 2006, the company had grown to a hundred employees. This team built a black version of the Roadster known as EP1, or "engineering prototype one." The arrival of the EP1 provided a great excuse to show existing investors what their money had bought and to ask for more funds from a wider audience. The investors were impressed enough to overlook the fact that engineers sometimes had to fan the car to cool it down in between test drives. Musk once again put money into Tesla—$12 million this time. A handful of other investors, including Larry Page and Sergey Brin, the Google founders, contributed and Tesla wound up with $40 million total.

In July 2006, Tesla decided to tell the world what it had been up to. The company's engineers had built a red prototype—EP2—to complement the black one, and they both went on display at an event in Santa Monica, California. The press flocked to the announcement and liked what they saw. The Roadsters were gorgeous, two-seater convertibles that could go from zero to sixty in about four seconds.

Celebrities like then–California governor Arnold Schwarzenegger and former Disney CEO Michael Eisner showed up at the event, and many of them took test rides in the Roadsters. The vehicles were so fragile that only Straubel and a couple of other trusted hands knew how to run them, and they were swapped out every five minutes to avoid overheating. Tesla revealed that each car would cost about $90,000 and have a range of 250 miles per charge. Thirty people, the company said, had committed to buying a Roadster, including the Google cofounders, Brin and Page, and a handful of other technology billionaires. Musk promised that a cheaper car—a four-seat, four-door model under $50,000—would arrive in about three years.

The month after the Santa Monica event was the Pebble Beach Concours d'Elegance, a famous showcase for exotic cars. Tesla had become such a topic of conversation that the organizers of the event begged to have a Roadster and waived the usual display fees. Tesla set up a booth, and people showed up by the dozens, writing $100,000 checks on the spot to preorder their cars.

"We just had not thought of trying to do that," Tarpenning said. "But then we started getting millions of dollars at these types of events." Investors, celebrities, and friends of Tesla employees began trying to buy their way onto the waiting list.

Quite often, the Tesla engineers applied their Silicon Valley attitude and methods to the car-making process and revamped many of the traditions in the auto industry. There's a brake and traction testing track in northern Sweden where cars get tuned on large plains of ice. It would be standard to run the car for three days or so, get the data, and return to company headquarters for many weeks of meetings about how to adjust the car. The whole process of tuning a car can take the entire winter. Tesla, by contrast, sent its engineers along with the Roadsters being tested and had them analyze the data on the spot. When something needed to be tweaked, the engineers would rewrite some code and send the car back on the ice.

Another testing procedure required that the Roadsters go into a special cooling chamber to check how they would respond to frigid temperatures. Not wanting to pay the enormous costs to use one of these chambers, the Tesla engineers decided to rent an ice cream delivery truck with a large refrigerated trailer. Someone would drive a Roadster into the truck, and the engineers would put on parkas and work on the car.

By the middle of 2007, Tesla had grown to 260 employees and seemed to be pulling off the impossible. It had produced the fastest, most beautiful electric car the world had ever seen, almost from thin air. All it had to do next was build a lot of the cars—a process that would end up almost bankrupting the company.

11

ROADSTER ROADBLOCKS

AS THE DIFFICULTIES OF BRINGING the Roadster to market worsened, Musk became more and more involved with Tesla. Musk had long influenced the design decisions of the company and overseen its operations as chairman. With each passing month, though, his business radar fired off alerts that Tesla needed more of Musk's personal supervision. Keeping Tesla alive would become one of his most formidable tests as a businessman.

The greatest mistake Tesla's executives made in the early days was assumptions around the transmission system for the Roadster. The goal had always been to get from zero to sixty mph as quickly as possible in the hopes that the raw

133

speed of the Roadster would make it fun to drive.

People had been making transmissions since the invention of the steam engine, so the Tesla engineers figured they could just order one. Time and again, however, the transmissions they received could not handle the big jump from first to second gear. Tesla had wanted to deliver the Roadster in November 2007, but the transmission issues lingered, and by the time January 1, 2008, rolled around, the company had to once again start from scratch, on what amounted to a third transmission push. Musk rolled up his sleeves and tackled this problem first.

Tesla also faced issues abroad. The company had decided to send a team of its youngest, most energetic engineers to Thailand to set up a battery factory. Their manufacturing partner had promised a state-of-the-art facility. Instead of a factory, the Tesla engineers found a concrete slab with posts holding up a roof and no proper walls. Tesla had sensitive batteries and electronics, and like parts of the Falcon 1, they'd be chewed up by the salty, humid conditions. The Tesla engineers had to convince their partner to put in drywall, coat the floor, and create storage rooms with temperature controls. Then the Tesla engineers needed to work crazy hours trying to train the Thai workers on how to handle the electronics properly.

The battery factory was one part of a supply chain that

stretched across the globe, adding cost and delays to the Roadster production. Body panels for the car were to be made in France, while the motors were to come from Taiwan. Tesla planned on buying battery cells in China and shipping them to Thailand to turn the piece parts into battery packs. The battery packs would then be shipped to England, where they needed to clear customs. Tesla then planned for Lotus to build the body of the car, attach the battery packs, and ship the Roadsters by boat around Cape Horn to Los Angeles.

"The idea was to get to Asia, get things done fast and cheap, and make money on the car," said Forrest North, one of the engineers sent to Thailand. "What we found out was that for really complicated things, you can do the work cheaper here and have less delays and less problems."

As word of the manufacturing issues reached Musk, he became very concerned about the way Eberhard had run the company, and called in a fixer to address the situation. One of Tesla's investors was Valor Equity, a Chicago-based investment firm that specialized in fine-tuning manufacturing operations. To protect its investment, Valor sent in Tim Watkins, its managing director of operations, and he soon reached some horrific conclusions.

Watkins was thorough and spent weeks talking to employees and analyzing every part of Tesla's supply chain to figure out how much it cost to make the Roadster. Around the middle of 2007, Watkins came to Musk with his findings. Musk was prepared for a high figure but felt confident that the price of the car would come down significantly over time as Tesla ironed out its manufacturing process and increased its sales. "That's when Tim told me it was really bad news," Musk said. It looked like each Roadster could cost up to $200,000 to make, and Tesla planned to sell the car for only around $85,000.

The ridiculous cost of the car, the transmission, and the ineffective suppliers were crippling Tesla. And, as the company started to miss its delivery dates, many of the consumers who had made their large up-front payments turned on Tesla and Eberhard.

Eberhard and Musk had battled for years over some of the design points on the car. But for the most part, they had gotten along well enough. What their relationship could not survive were the cost figures for the Roadster unearthed by Watkins. It looked to Musk as if Eberhard had mismanaged the company by allowing the parts costs to soar so high. Then, as Musk saw it, Eberhard had failed to disclose the severity of the situation to the board. While on his way to give a talk in Los Angeles, Eberhard received a call from Musk and in a brief, uncomfortable chat learned that he would be replaced as CEO.

Eberhard had already been asking Tesla's board to replace him as CEO and find someone with more manufacturing experience. The way he was demoted, however, angered him. By December, the situation had only gotten worse, and Eberhard left the company altogether.

As 2007 played out, the problems mounted for Tesla. The carbon-fiber body that looked so good turned out to be a huge pain to paint. Sometimes there were faults in the battery pack. The motor short-circuited now and again. The body panels had visible gaps. The company also had to face up to the reality that the planned transmission was not going to happen. Instead, Tesla's engineers had to redesign the car's motor and inverter—a component that turns direct current into alternating current—and shave off some weight in order for the Roadster to achieve its flashy zero-to-sixty times with a different type of transmission. "We essentially had to do a complete reboot," Musk said. "That was terrible."

After Eberhard was removed as CEO, Tesla's board tapped Michael Marks as its interim chief. Marks had run an enormous electronics supplier and had deep experience with complex manufacturing operations. Tesla moved into a larger facility in San Carlos. The bigger building allowed Tesla to bring the battery work back in-house from Asia. Tesla also began to do some of the Roadster manufacturing there, alleviating the supply chain issues.

Marks recommended selling Tesla to a larger car company. It was a perfectly reasonable plan. Tesla must have looked borderline hopeless to Marks at this point. The company could not make its one product well, was poised to lose vast amounts of money, and had missed a string of delivery deadlines. Making Tesla look as pretty as possible for a buyer was the rational thing to do.

In just about every other case, Marks would be thanked for his decisive plan of action and saving the company's investors from a big loss. But Musk had little interest in polishing up Tesla's assets for the highest bidder. He'd started the company to put a dent in the automotive industry and force people to rethink electric cars. "The product was late and over budget and everything was wrong, but Elon didn't want anything to do with those plans to either sell the whole company or lose control through a partnership," Straubel said. On December 3, 2007, Ze'ev Drori replaced Marks as CEO.

While the customers complained a lot about the delays, they seemed to share Musk's enthusiasm for the product. Only a handful of customers asked for their prepayments back.

Tesla employees soon got to witness the same Musk that SpaceX employees had seen for years. When an issue like the Roadster's faulty carbon-fiber body panels cropped up, Musk dealt with it directly. He flew to England in his jet to pick up some new manufacturing tools for the body panels and personally delivered them to a factory in France to ensure that the Roadster stayed on its production schedule.

Musk also instituted a new intense cost-tracking system. "Elon . . . gave a speech, saying we would work on Saturdays and Sundays and sleep under desks until it got done," said Ryan Popple, the director of finance at Tesla. "Someone pushed back from the table and argued that everyone had been working so hard just to get the car done, and they were ready for a break and to see their families. Elon said, 'I would tell those people they will get to see their families a lot when we go bankrupt.' I was like, 'Wow,' but I got it. I had come out of a military culture, and you just have to make your objective happen."

Everyone quickly understood that Musk meant business. Marketing people were let go, as were other people who hadn't done anything "awesome" in recent memory. "He can be incredibly intimidating at times but doesn't have a real sense for just how imposing he can be," said one former Tesla executive. The employees would take bets on who Musk would target next.

Straubel welcomed Musk's hard-charging presence. Over the past five years, Straubel had emerged as the most crucial member of the technical team. He knew more about the batteries and the electric drivetrain than anyone else at the company. All that mattered to Straubel was getting the Roadster and the follow-on sedan to market to popularize electric cars, and Musk looked like the best person to make that happen.

Other employees had enjoyed the thrill of the engineering challenge over the past five years but were burnt-out beyond repair. Wright left and started his own company to make electric versions of delivery trucks. Berdichevsky had been a crucial, do-anything young engineer for much of Tesla's existence. Now that the company employed about three hundred people, he felt less effective and didn't like the idea of suffering for another five years to bring the sedan to market. He left, and with Eberhard gone, Tarpenning found Tesla less fun. He didn't see eye to eye with the new CEO, Drori, and also didn't like the idea of spending his every waking hour to get the sedan out, so he bolted too.

Tesla could survive the loss of some of these early hires. Its strong brand had allowed the company to keep recruiting top talent, including people from large automotive companies who knew how to get over the last set of challenges blocking the Roadster from reaching customers. But Tesla's major issue no longer revolved around effort, engineering, or clever marketing. Heading into 2008, the company was running out of money. The Roadster had cost about $140 million to develop, way over the $25 million originally estimated in the 2004 business plan.

Under normal circumstances, Tesla had probably done enough to raise more funds. These, however, were not normal times. The big automakers in the United States were charging toward bankruptcy in the middle of the worst financial crisis since the Great Depression. In the midst of all this, Musk needed to convince Tesla's investors to fork over tens of millions of additional dollars. As Musk put it, "Try to imagine explaining that you're investing in an electric car company, and everything you read about the car company sounds like it is . . . doomed and it's a recession and no one is buying cars." All Musk had to do to dig Tesla out of this problem was lose his entire fortune and verge on an emotional meltdown.

12

PAIN, SUFFERING, AND SURVIVAL

AS HE PREPARED TO BEGIN filming *Iron Man* in early 2007, director Jon Favreau rented out a complex in Los Angeles that once belonged to aerospace and defense contractor Hughes Aircraft. The facility had a series of interlocking hangars, which supplied Robert Downey Jr., who was to play Iron Man and his human creator, Tony Stark, with a splash of inspiration. Downey felt nostalgic looking at one of the larger hangars, which had fallen into a state of disrepair. Not too long ago, that building had played host to the big ideas of business tycoon and aerospace daredevil Howard Hughes, a man who shook up industries and did things his own way.

Downey heard some rumblings about a Hughes-like figure named Elon Musk, who had constructed his own, modern-day industrial complex about ten miles away. Instead of visualizing how life might have been for Hughes, Downey could perhaps get a taste of the real thing. He set off in March 2007 for SpaceX's headquarters in El Segundo and wound up receiving a personal tour of the facility from Musk. "My mind is not easily blown, but this place and this guy were amazing," Downey said.

To Downey, the SpaceX factory looked like a giant, exotic hardware store. Enthusiastic employees were zipping about, fiddling with an assortment of machines. Young engineers interacted with assembly line workers, and they all seemed to share a genuine excitement for what they were doing. "It felt like a radical start-up company," Downey said. After the initial tour, Downey came away pleased that the movie sets being hammered out at the Hughes factory did have parallels to the SpaceX factory. "Things didn't feel out of place," he said.

Beyond the surroundings, Downey really wanted a peek inside Musk's psyche. The men walked, sat in Musk's office, and had lunch. Downey appreciated that Musk was not a foul-smelling, fidgety coder whack job. What Downey picked up on instead were Musk's "accessible eccentricities" and the feeling that he was an unpretentious sort who could work alongside the people in the factory. Both Musk and Stark were the type of men, according to Downey, who "had seized an idea to live by and something to dedicate themselves to" and were not going to waste a moment.

When he returned to the *Iron Man* production office, Downey asked that Favreau be sure to place a Tesla Roadster in Tony Stark's workshop. On a superficial level, this would symbolize that Stark was so cool and connected that he could get a Roadster before it even went on sale. On a deeper level, the car was to be placed as the nearest object to Stark's desk so that it formed something of a bond between the actor, the character, and Musk. "After meeting Elon . . . I felt like having his presence in the workshop," Downey said. "They became contemporaries. Elon was someone Tony probably hung out with."

After *Iron Man* came out, Favreau began talking up Musk's role as the inspiration for Downey's interpretation of Tony Stark. It was a stretch on many levels, but the press lapped up the comparison, and Musk started to become more of a public figure thanks to it. People who sort of knew him as "that PayPal guy" began to think of him as the rich, eccentric businessman behind SpaceX and Tesla.

Musk enjoyed his rising reputation. It fed his ego and provided some fun. He and Justine bought a house in Bel Air. Musk and some former PayPal executives produced a movie. Musk reveled in the Hollywood nightlife. "There were just a lot of parties to go to," said Bill Lee, Musk's close friend. "Elon was neighbors with two quasi celebrities. Our friends were making movies and through this confluence of our networks, there was something to go out and do every night."

Justine appeared to enjoy their status even more than Musk. She kept a blog about the couple's family life and their adventures on the town. In one entry, Justine wrote about meeting Leonardo DiCaprio at a club and having him beg for a free Tesla Roadster, only to be turned down. In another entry, she said that Musk would like to visit a Chuck E. Cheese sometime.

The press had not run into a guy like Musk for a very long time. His shine as an internet millionaire kept getting, well, shinier thanks to PayPal's ongoing success. He also had an element of mystery. There was the weird name. And there was the willingness to spend huge sums of money on spaceships and electric cars.

The press had picked up on the fact that Musk tended to talk a huge game and then struggle to deliver on his promises in time, but they didn't much care. The game he talked was so much bigger than anyone else's that reporters were comfortable giving Musk leeway. Silicon Valley's bloggers praised Tesla's every move. Similarly, reporters covering SpaceX were overjoyed that a young, feisty company had arrived to needle Boeing, Lockheed, and, to a large extent, NASA.

While Musk put on a good show for the public and press, he'd started to get very worried about his businesses. SpaceX's second launch attempt had failed, and the reports coming in from Tesla kept getting worse. Musk had started these two adventures with a fortune nearing $200 million and had chewed through more than half the money with little to show for it. As each Tesla delay turned into a press fiasco, the Musk glow dimmed. People in Silicon Valley began to gossip about Musk's money problems. Reporters who months earlier had been praising Musk turned on him. The *New York Times* picked up on Tesla's transmission problems. Automotive websites complained that the Roadster might never ship. By the end of 2007, things got downright nasty. Valleywag, Silicon Valley's gossip blog, dubbed the Tesla Roadster its number one fail of 2007 among technology companies.

As his businesses and public persona suffered, Musk's home life degraded as well. His triplets—Kai, Damian, and Saxon—had arrived near the end of 2006 and joined their twin brothers Griffin and Xavier, but Musk said, "In the spring of 2007, our marriage was having real issues." Justine's blog posts described a much less romantic Musk than the guy from their early days together, and she felt people didn't treat her with equal respect to her husband.

As 2007 rolled into 2008, Musk's life became more difficult. Tesla basically had to start over on much of the Roadster, and SpaceX still had dozens of people living in Kwajalein awaiting the next launch of the Falcon 1. Both endeavors were vacuuming up Musk's money. He started selling off prized possessions like the McLaren sports car to generate extra cash.

Musk tended to shield employees from the seriousness of his financial situation by always encouraging them to do their best work. At the same time, he personally oversaw all significant purchases at both companies. Musk also trained employees to make the right trade-offs between spending money and productivity. This struck many of the SpaceX employees as a novel idea, since they were used to traditional aerospace companies that had huge, multiyear government contracts and no day-to-day survival pressure.

"Elon would always be at work on Sunday, and we had some chats where he laid out his philosophy," said Kevin Brogan, an early SpaceX employee. "He would say that everything we did was a function of our burn rate and that we were burning through a hundred thousand dollars per day. It was this very entrepreneurial, Silicon Valley way of thinking that none of the aerospace engineers in Los

Angeles were dialed into. Sometimes he wouldn't let you buy a part for two thousand dollars because he expected you to find it cheaper or invent something cheaper. Other times, he wouldn't flinch at renting a plane for ninety thousand dollars to get something to Kwaj because it saved an entire workday, so it was worth it."

In the first half of 2008, Antonio Gracias, the founder and CEO of Valor Equity, met Musk for dinner. Gracias had been an investor in Tesla and had become one of Musk's closest friends. He could see Musk worrying about his future. "Things were starting to be difficult with Justine, but they were still together," Gracias said. "During that dinner, Elon said, 'I will spend my last dollar on these companies. If we have to move into Justine's parents' basement, we'll do it.'" But that option expired on June 16, 2008, when Musk filed for divorce.

In the weeks after, Musk tumbled into a deep funk. Bill Lee started to worry about his friend's mental state and, as one of Musk's more free-spirited friends, wanted to do something to cheer him up. Now and again, Musk and Lee, a technology entrepreneur and investor, would take trips overseas and mix business and pleasure. The time was right for just such a journey, and they set off for London at the start of July.

The trip began poorly. Musk and Lee visited the

headquarters of Aston Martin to see the company's CEO and get a tour of his factory. The executive treated Musk like an amateur car builder. Then, Musk had a nagging stomach pain turn severe. They thought that Musk might be suffering from appendicitis, and Lee took him to a medical clinic. When the tests came back negative, Lee set to work trying to pressure Musk into a night on the town. "Elon didn't want to go out, and I didn't really either," Lee said. "But I was like, 'No, come on. We're all the way here.'"

Lee coaxed Musk into going to a club. People had packed the small dance spot, and Musk wanted to leave after ten minutes. The well-connected Lee texted a promoter friend of his, who pulled some strings to get Musk escorted into the VIP area. The promoter then reached out to some of his prettiest friends, including a twenty-two-year-old actress named Talulah Riley, and they soon arrived at the club as well. Riley and her two friends had come from a charity gala and were in full-length, flowing gowns. Musk and Riley were introduced by people at the club, and he perked up at the sight of her.

Musk and Riley sat at a table with their friends but immediately focused on each other. Riley had just hit it big with her portrayal of Mary Bennet in *Pride and Prejudice* and thought of herself as quite the hotshot. Musk whipped out his phone and displayed photos of the Falcon 1 and the

Roadster. Riley thought he had just done some work on the rocket and car and didn't realize he ran the companies building them. "I remember thinking that this guy probably didn't get to talk to young actresses a lot and that he seemed quite nervous," Riley said. "I decided to be really nice to him and give him a nice evening. Little did I know that he'd spoken to a lot of pretty girls in his life."

While Musk thought Riley did look great, he was more impressed that she was willing to discuss rockets and electric cars with him. The more Musk and Riley talked, the more Lee egged them on. It was the first time in weeks that his friend had appeared happy. Musk asked Riley out to dinner the next night, and she accepted.

Once Musk went back to the United States, they kept in touch via email for a couple of weeks, and then Riley booked a flight to Los Angeles. Riley had been in California for just five days when he made his move. "He said, 'I don't want you to leave. I want you to marry me.' I think I laughed. Then he said, 'No. I'm serious. I'm sorry I don't have a ring.' I said, 'We can shake on it if you like.' And we did. I don't remember what I was thinking at the time, and all I can say is that I was twenty-two."

The whirlwind romance had given Riley the impression that she was engaged to a world-conquering, jet-setting billionaire. That was true in theory but less so in practice.

As late July rolled around, Musk could see that he had just enough cash on hand to scrape through to the end of the year. Both SpaceX and Tesla would need cash infusions at some point just to pay the employees, and it was unclear where that money would come from with the world's financial markets collapsing. If things had been going more smoothly at the companies, Musk could have felt more confident about raising money, but they were not. "He would come home every day, and there would be some calamity," Riley said. "He was under immense pressure from all quarters. It was horrendous."

SpaceX's third flight from Kwajalein jumped out as Musk's most pressing concern. His team of engineers had remained camped out on the island, preparing the Falcon 1 for another run. A typical company would focus just on the task at hand. Not SpaceX. It had shipped the Falcon 1 to Kwaj in April with one set of engineers and then put another group of engineers on a new project to develop the Falcon 9, a nine-engine rocket that would take the place of the Falcon 5 and serve as a possible replacement to the retiring space shuttle. SpaceX had yet to prove it could get to space successfully, but Musk kept positioning it to bid on big-ticket NASA contracts.

On July 30, 2008, the Falcon 9 had a successful test fire in Texas with all nine of its engines lighting up and producing 850,000 pounds of thrust. Three days later, in Kwaj, SpaceX's engineers fueled up the Falcon 1 and crossed their fingers. The rocket had an air force satellite as its payload, along with a couple of experiments from NASA. All told, the cargo weighed 375 pounds. SpaceX had been making significant changes to its rocket since the last, failed launch. A traditional aerospace company would not have wanted the added risk, but Musk insisted that SpaceX push its technology forward while at the same time trying to make it work right. Among the biggest changes for the Falcon 1 was a new version of the Merlin 1 engine that relied on a tweaked cooling system.

The first launch attempt on August 2, 2008, aborted at T-minus zero seconds. SpaceX regrouped and tried to launch again the same day. This time everything seemed to be going well. The Falcon 1 soared into the sky and flew spectacularly without any indication of a problem. SpaceX employees watching a webcast of the proceedings back in California let out hoots and whistles. Then, right at the moment when the first stage and second stage were to separate, there was a malfunction and another catastrophe. An analysis after the fact would show that the new engines had delivered an unexpected thrust during the separation process that caused the first stage to bump up into the second stage, damaging the top part of the rocket and its engine.

The failed launch left many SpaceX employees shattered. "It was so profound seeing the energy shift over the room in the course of thirty seconds," said Dolly Singh, a recruiter at SpaceX. "It was like the worst . . . day ever. You don't usually see grown-ups weeping, but there they were. We were tired and broken emotionally." Musk addressed the workers right away and encouraged them to get back to work. "He said, 'Look. We are going to do this. It's going to be okay. Don't freak out,'" Singh recalled. "It was like magic. Everyone chilled out immediately and started to focus on figuring out what just happened and how to fix it. It went from despair to hope and focus." Musk put up a positive front to the public as well. In a statement, he said that SpaceX had another rocket waiting to attempt a fourth launch and a fifth launch planned shortly after that. "I have also given the go-ahead to begin fabrication of flight six," he said. "Falcon 9 development will also continue unabated."

In reality, the third launch was a disaster that came with ongoing consequences. Since the second stage of the rocket did not fire properly, SpaceX never got a chance to see if it had really fixed the fuel-sloshing issues that had plagued the second flight. Many of the SpaceX engineers were confident that they had solved this problem and were anxious to get to the fourth launch. They also thought they had an easy answer for the recent thrust problem.

For Musk, the situation seemed graver. "I was super-depressed," Musk said. "If we hadn't solved the slosh coupling problem on flight two, or there was just some random other thing that occurred—say, a mistake in the launch process or the manufacturing process unrelated to anything previous—then game over." SpaceX simply did not have enough money to try a fifth flight. He'd put $100 million into the company and had nothing to spare because of the issues at Tesla. "Flight four was it," Musk said.

The fourth and possibly final launch for SpaceX took place on September 28, 2008. The SpaceX employees had worked nonstop shifts under agonizing pressure for six weeks to reach this day. Their pride as engineers and their hopes and dreams were on the line. "The people watching back at the factory were trying their best not to throw up," said James McLaury, a metrology manager at SpaceX. Despite their past flubs, the engineers on Kwaj were confident that this launch would work. Some of these people had spent years on the island going through one of the more surreal engineering exercises in human history. They had been separated from their families, assaulted by the heat, and exiled on their tiny launchpad outpost—sometimes without much food—for days on end as they waited for the launch windows to open and dealt with the aborts that followed. So much of that pain and suffering and fear would be forgotten if this launch went successfully.

In the late afternoon on the twenty-eighth, the SpaceX team raised the Falcon 1 into its launch position. Once again, it stood tall, looking like a bizarre artifact of an island tribe as palm trees swayed beside it and a smattering of clouds crossed through the spectacular blue sky. The Falcon 1 was not carrying real cargo this time; neither the company nor the military wanted to see something else blow up or get lost at sea, so the rocket held a 360-pound dummy payload.

The fact that SpaceX had been reduced to launch theatrics did not faze the employees or dampen their enthusiasm. As the rocket rumbled and then climbed higher, the employees back at SpaceX headquarters let out raucous cheers. Each milestone that followed—clearing the island, engine checks coming back good—was again met with whistles and shouts. As the first stage fell away, the second stage fired up about ninety seconds into the flight and the employees turned downright rapturous, filling the webcast with their ecstatic hollering. "Perfect," said one of the talking heads on the webcast. The Kestrel engine glowed red and started its six-minute burn. "When the second stage cleared, I could finally start breathing again and my knees stopped buckling," said McLaury.

The fairing opened up, releasing the payload, around

the three-minute mark and fell back toward Earth. And, finally, around nine minutes into its journey, the Falcon 1 shut down just as planned and reached orbit, making it the first privately built machine to accomplish such a feat. It took six years—about four and half more than Musk had once planned—and five hundred people to make this miracle of modern science and business happen.

SpaceX built a mobile mission-control trailer, and Musk and Mueller used it to monitor the later launches from Kwaj. Photograph courtesy of SpaceX

Earlier in the day, Musk had tried to distract himself from the mounting pressure by going to Disneyland with his brother, Kimbal, and their children. Musk then had to race back to make the four p.m. launch and walked into SpaceX's trailer control room about two minutes before blastoff. "When the launch was successful, everyone burst into tears," Kimbal said. Musk left the control room and walked out to the factory floor, where he received a rock star's welcome.

"Well, that was freaking awesome," he said. "There are a lot of people who thought we couldn't do it—a lot, actually—but as the saying goes, 'the fourth time is the charm,' right? There are only a handful of countries on Earth that have done this. It's normally a country thing, not a company thing . . . My mind is kind of frazzled, so it's hard for me to say anything, but, man, this is definitely one of the greatest days in my life, and I think probably for most people here. We showed people we can do it. This is just the first step of many . . ."

The afterglow of this mammoth victory faded soon after the party ended, and the severity of SpaceX's financial trouble became top of mind again for Musk. SpaceX had the Falcon 9 efforts to support and had also immediately green-lighted the construction of another machine—the Dragon capsule—that would be used to take supplies, and one day humans, to the International Space Station. Historically, either project would cost more than $1 billion to complete, but SpaceX would have to find a way to build both machines for a fraction of the cost. The company had dramatically increased the rate at which it hired employees and moved into a much larger headquarters in Hawthorne. SpaceX had a commercial flight booked to carry a satellite into orbit for the Malaysian government, but that launch and the payment for it would not arrive until the middle of 2009. In the meantime, SpaceX simply struggled to make its payroll.

SpaceX's ambitions grew over the years to include the construction of the Dragon capsule, which could take people to the International Space Station and beyond. © Steve Jurvetson

The press did not know the extent of Musk's financial problems, but they knew enough to turn their focus to Tesla's dangerous financial situation. A website called The Truth About Cars began a "Tesla Death Watch" in May 2008. *Top Gear*, a popular British television show, ripped the Roadster apart. "People joke about the Tesla Death Watch and all that, but it was harsh," said Kimbal Musk. "One day there were fifty articles about how Tesla will die."

Yes, Tesla deserved much of the negative attention because of its delays and high costs. Musk, though, felt like the 2008 climate—filled with hatred for bankers and the rich—had turned him into a particularly juicy target. "I was just getting pistol-whipped," Musk said. "[I]t was bad on so many levels. Justine was torturing me in the press. There were always all these negative articles about Tesla, and the stories about SpaceX's third failure. It hurt really bad. You have these huge doubts that your life is not working, your car is not working, you're going through a divorce, and all of those things. . . . I didn't think we would overcome it. I thought things were probably . . . doomed."

When Musk ran through the calculations concerning SpaceX and Tesla, it occurred to him that only one company would likely have a chance at survival. "I could either pick SpaceX or Tesla or split the money I had left between them," Musk said. "That was a tough decision. If I split the money, maybe both of them would die. If I gave the money to just one company, the probability of it surviving was greater, but then it would mean certain death for the other company. I debated that over and over." As 2008 came to an end, Musk had run out of money.

Because of the long hours that he worked and his eating habits, Musk's weight fluctuated wildly. Bags formed under his eyes, and he began to look like a shattered runner at the end of an ultramarathon. "He looked like death itself," Riley said. "I remember thinking this guy would have a heart attack and die." The couple had to borrow hundreds of thousands of dollars from Musk's billionaire friend Jeff Skoll. Musk no longer flew his jet back and forth between Los Angles and Silicon Valley. He took Southwest.

Burning through about $4 million a month, Tesla needed to close another major round of funding to get through 2008 and stay alive. Musk had to lean on friends just to try to make payroll from week to week as he negotiated with investors. He sent impassioned pleas to anyone he could think of who might be able to spare some money. Bill Lee invested $2 million in Tesla, and Sergey Brin invested $500,000. "A bunch of Tesla employees wrote checks to keep the company going," said Diarmuid O'Connell, the vice president of business development at Tesla. "They turned into investments, but, at the time, it was twenty-five or fifty thousand dollars that you didn't expect to see again. It just seemed like . . . this thing is going to crater."

Kimbal had lost most of his money during the recession when his investments bottomed out, but sold what he had left and put it into Tesla as well. "I was close to bankruptcy," Kimbal said. Tesla had set the prepayments that customers made for the Roadsters aside, but Musk now needed to use that money to keep the company going, and soon those funds were gone too. These fiscal maneuvers worried Kimbal. "I'm sure Elon would have found a way to make things right, but he definitely took risks that seemed like they could have landed him in jail for using someone else's money," he said.

In December 2008, Musk started several campaigns to try to save his companies. He heard a rumor that NASA was on the verge of awarding a contract to resupply the space station. SpaceX's fourth launch had put it in a position to receive some of this money, which was said to be more than $1 billion.

Musk found out that SpaceX might even be a front-runner for the deal. Musk began doing everything in his power to assure people that the company could meet the challenge of getting a capsule to the ISS. As for Tesla, Musk had to go to his existing investors and ask them for another round of funding that needed to close by Christmas Eve to avoid bankruptcy. To give the investors some measure of confidence, Musk made a last-ditch effort to raise all the personal funds he could and put them into the company. He took out a loan from SpaceX and earmarked the money for Tesla. Musk tried to sell some of his shares in SolarCity. He also received about $15 million that came through when Dell bought a data center software start-up called Everdream, founded by Musk's cousins, in which he had invested. "It was like the . . . Matrix," Musk said, describing his financial maneuvers. "The Everdream deal really saved my butt."

Musk had cobbled together $20 million, and asked Tesla's existing investors—since no new investors materialized—to match that figure. The investors agreed, and on December 3, 2008, they were in the process of finalizing the paperwork for the funding round when Musk noticed a problem. VantagePoint Capital Partners had signed all of the paperwork except for one crucial page. Musk phoned up Alan Salzman, VantagePoint's cofounder and managing partner, to ask about the situation. Salzman informed Musk that the firm had a problem with the investment round because it undervalued Tesla. Musk replied, "I've got an excellent solution, then. Take my entire portion of the deal. I had a real hard time coming up with the money. Based on the cash we have in the bank right now, we will bounce payroll next week. So unless you've got another idea, can you either just participate as much as you'd like, or allow the round to go through because otherwise we will be bankrupt?"

Salzman hesitated and told Musk to come in the following week at seven a.m. to present to VantagePoint's top people. Not having a week of time to work with, Musk asked to come in the next day. Salzman refused that offer, forcing Musk to continue taking on loans. "The only reason he wanted the meeting at his office was for me to come on bended knee begging for money so he could say, 'No,'" Musk theorized.

VantagePoint declined to speak about this period, but Musk believed that Salzman's tactics were part of a mission to bankrupt Tesla. Musk feared that VantagePoint would remove him as CEO and sell Tesla to a Detroit automaker or focus on selling electric drivetrains and battery packs instead of making cars. Such reasoning would have been quite practical from a business standpoint but did not match up with Musk's goals for Tesla.

"VantagePoint was forcing that wisdom down the throat of an entrepreneur who wanted to do something bigger and bolder," said Steve Jurvetson, a partner at the investment firm Draper Fisher Jurvetson who had put money into Tesla. "Maybe they're used to a CEO buckling, but Elon doesn't do that."

With the help of Antonio Gracias from Valor Equity, Musk eventually won over Tesla's major investors, and they were able to prevent VantagePoint from disrupting any deals. Tesla secured its $40 million funding round and saved the company—for the time being.

The deal ended up closing on Christmas Eve, hours before Tesla would have gone bankrupt. Musk had just a few hundred thousand dollars left and could not have made payroll the next day. Musk ultimately put in $12 million, and the investment firms put up the rest. As for Salzman, Musk said, "He should be ashamed of himself."

At SpaceX, Musk and the company's top executives had spent most of December terrified. According to reports in the press, SpaceX, the onetime front-runner for the large NASA contract, had suddenly lost favor with the space agency. Michael Griffin, who had once almost been a cofounder of SpaceX, was the head of NASA and had turned on Musk. Griffin did not care for Musk's aggressive business tactics, seeing him as borderline unethical. Others have suggested that Griffin ended up being jealous of Musk and SpaceX.

On December 23, 2008, however, SpaceX received a shock. People inside NASA had worked around Griffin and backed SpaceX to become a supplier for the ISS. The company received $1.6 billion as payment for twelve flights to the space station. Staying with Kimbal in Boulder, Colorado, for the holidays, Musk broke down in tears as the SpaceX and Tesla transactions processed.

13

LIFT-OFF

THE FALCON 9 HAS BECOME SpaceX's go-to rocket. It stands 224.4 feet tall, is twelve feet across, and weighs 1.1 million pounds. The rocket is powered by nine engines arranged in an "octaweb" pattern at its base with one engine in the center and eight others encircling it. The engines connect to the first stage, or the main body of the rocket, which bears the blue SpaceX insignia and an American flag. The shorter, second stage of the rocket sits on top of the first and is the one that actually ends up doing things in space. It can be outfitted with a rounded container for carrying satellites or a capsule capable of transporting humans. There's nothing particularly flashy about the Falcon 9's outward appearance. It's an elegant, purposeful machine.

About four hours before a launch, the Falcon 9 starts getting filled with an immense amount of liquid oxygen and rocket-grade kerosene. Some of the liquid oxygen escapes the rocket as it awaits launch and is kept so cold that it boils off on contact with the metal and air.

The engineers inside of SpaceX's mission control monitor these fuel systems and all manner of other items. They chat back and forth through headsets and begin cycling through their launch checklist, consumed by what people in the business call "go fever" as they move from one approval to the next. Ten minutes before launch, the humans step out of the way and leave the remaining processes up to automated machines. Everything goes quiet, and the tension builds until right before the main event. That's when, out of nowhere, the Falcon 9 breaks the silence by letting out a loud gasp.

A white support structure pulls away from the rocket's body. The T-minus-ten-seconds countdown begins. Nothing much happens from ten down to four. At the count of three, however, the engines ignite, and the computers conduct a last, oh-so-rapid health check. Four enormous metal clamps hold the rocket down as computing systems evaluate all nine engines and measure if there's sufficient downward force being produced. By the time zero arrives, the rocket has decided that all is well enough to go through with its mission, and the clamps release.

The rocket shoots up with flames surrounding its base and snow-thick streaks of the liquid oxygen filling the air. About twenty seconds after liftoff, the spectators placed safely a few miles away catch the first faceful of the Falcon 9's rumble. Pant legs vibrate from shock waves produced by a stream of sonic booms coming out of the Falcon 9's exhaust. The white rocket climbs higher and higher with impressive stamina. After about a minute, it's just a red spot in the sky, and then—poof—it's gone.

For Elon Musk, this spectacle has turned into a familiar experience. SpaceX has changed from the joke of the aeronautics industry into one of its most consistent operators. SpaceX sends a rocket up about once a month, carrying satellites for companies and nations and supplies to the International Space Station. Where the Falcon 1 blasting off from Kwajalein was the work of a start-up, the Falcon 9 taking off from Vandenberg is the work of an aerospace superpower. SpaceX can undercut its US competitors—Boeing, Lockheed Martin, Orbital Sciences—on price by a ridiculous margin.

It also offers US customers a peace of mind that its rivals can't. Where these competitors rely on Russian and other foreign suppliers, SpaceX makes all of its machines from scratch in the United States. Because of its low costs,

SpaceX has once again made the United States a player in the worldwide commercial launch market. Its $60 million per launch cost is much less than what Europe and Japan charge and beats even the relative bargains offered by the Russians and the Chinese.

The United States government leaders and the public have been willing to concede much of the market for sending satellites and supplies to space. It's a disheartening and shortsighted position. The total market for satellites, related services, and the rocket launches needed to carry them to space has exploded over the past decade. A number of countries pay to send up their own spy, communication, and weather satellites. Companies then turn to space for television, internet, radio, weather, navigation, and imaging services. The machines in space are part of modern life, and they're becoming more capable and interesting at a rapid pace.

The retirement of the space shuttle made the United States totally dependent on the Russians to get astronauts to the ISS. Russia charges $70 million per person for the trip and can cut the United States off as it sees fit during political rifts. At present, SpaceX looks like the best hope of breaking this cycle and returning America's ability to take people into space.

SpaceX is trying to upend everything about this

industry. Musk's goal is to use manufacturing break-throughs and launchpad advances to create a drastic drop in the cost of getting things to space. Most significant, he's been testing rockets that can push their payload to space and then return to Earth and land with accuracy on a pad floating at sea or even their original launchpad. Instead of having its rockets break apart after crashing into the sea, SpaceX will use reverse thrusters to lower them down softly and reuse them. Within the next few years, SpaceX expects to cut its price to at least one-tenth that of its rivals by developing these reusable rockets, while its competitors continue to throw their spaceships away after each launch.

SpaceX hopes to take over the majority of the world's commercial launches, and there's evidence that the company is on its way toward doing just that. To date, it has flown satellites for Canadian, European, and Asian customers and completed about two dozen launches. Its public launch schedule stretches out for a number of years, and SpaceX has more than fifty flights planned, which are all together worth more than $5 billion. Since getting past its near-death experience in 2008, SpaceX has been profitable and is estimated to be worth $10 billion.

Musk does not simply want to lower the cost of sending up satellites and resupplying the space station. He wants to lower the cost of launches to the point that it becomes economical to fly thousands upon thousands of supply trips to Mars and start a colony. Musk wants to conquer the solar system, and, as it stands, there's just one company where you can work if that sort of mission gets you out of bed in the morning.

The SpaceX hiring model places some emphasis on getting top marks at top schools. But most of the attention goes toward spotting engineers who ooze passion, can work well as part of a team, and have real-world experience bending metal. "Even if you're someone who writes code for your job, you need to understand how mechanical things work," said Dolly Singh, who spent five years as the head of talent acquisition at SpaceX. "We were looking for people who had been building things since they were little."

Like many tech companies, SpaceX subjects potential hires to all manner of interviews and tests. The reward for solving the puzzles, acting clever in interviews, and penning up a good essay is a meeting with Musk. He interviewed almost every one of SpaceX's first one thousand hires, including the janitors and technicians, and has continued to interview the engineers.

Each employee receives a warning before going to meet with Musk. The interview, he or she is told, could last anywhere from thirty seconds to fifteen minutes. Elon will likely keep on writing emails and working during the initial part of the interview and not speak much. Don't panic. That's normal. Eventually, he will turn around in his chair to face you. Even then, though, he might not make actual eye contact with you or fully acknowledge your presence. Don't panic. That's normal. In due course, he will speak to you.

From that point, Musk might ask one question or he might ask several. You can be sure, though, that he will roll out the riddle: "You're standing on the surface of the Earth. You walk one mile south, one mile west, and one mile north. You end up exactly where you started. Where are you?" Spoiler alert: one answer to that is the North Pole, and most of the engineers get it right away. That's when Musk will follow with "Where else could you be?" The other answer is somewhere close to the South Pole, where, if you walk one mile south, the circumference of the earth becomes one mile. Fewer engineers get this answer. Musk tends to care less about whether or not the person gets the answer than about how they describe the problem and their approach to solving it.

When speaking to potential recruits, Singh tried to energize them and be up front about the demands of SpaceX and of Musk at the same time. "The recruiting pitch was 'SpaceX is special forces,'" she said. "If you want as hard as it gets, then great. If not, then you shouldn't come here." Once at SpaceX, the new employees found out very quickly if they were indeed up for the challenge. Many of them would quit within the first few months because of the ninety-plus-hour workweeks. Others quit because they could not handle just how direct Musk and the other executives were during meetings. "Elon doesn't know about you and he hasn't thought through whether or not something is going to hurt your feelings," Singh said. "He just knows what . . . he wants done. People who did not normalize to his communication style did not do well."

For those who like the challenge and can handle the blunt speech, SpaceX and Musk seem to inspire an unusual level of loyalty. Musk is very good at exciting his troops. "His vision is so clear," Singh said. "He almost hypnotizes you. He gives you the crazy eye, and it's like, yes, we can get to Mars."

SpaceX's original headquarters in El Segundo were not quite up to the company's desired image as a place where the cool kids want to work. This is not a problem for SpaceX's new facility in Hawthorne at 1 Rocket Road. The all-white SpaceX building looks like a huge, rectangular glacier that's been planted in the midst of Los Angeles County's sprawl.

When SpaceX moved to a new factory in Hawthorne, California, it was able to scale out its assembly line and work on multiple rockets and capsules at the same time. © Steve Jurvetson

The SpaceX front doors are reflective and hide what's on the inside. After going through the registration process, guests are led into the main SpaceX office space. Musk's cubicle—a supersize unit—sits to the right, where he has a couple of *Aviation Week* magazine covers up on the wall, pictures of his boys, and various knickknacks on his desk, including a boomerang and a giant samurai sword named Lady Vivamus. Hundreds of other people work in cubicles amid the big, wide-open area, most of them executives, engineers, software developers, and salespeople tapping away on their computers.

Take away the rocket swag and the samurai sword, and this central part of the SpaceX office looks just like what you might find at any Silicon Valley headquarters. The same thing cannot be said for what visitors encounter as they pass through a pair of double doors into the heart of the SpaceX factory.

The 550,000-square-foot factory floor is one continuous space with grayish floors, white walls, and white support columns. A small city's worth of stuff—people, machines, noise—has been piled into this area. Just near the entryway, one of the Dragon capsules that has gone to the ISS and returned to Earth hangs from the ceiling with black burn marks running down its side. Right under the capsule on the ground are a pair of the twenty-five-foot-long landing legs built by SpaceX to let the Falcon rocket come to a gentle landing after a flight so it can be flown again. To the right side of the entryway area, there's the mission control room. It's a closed-off space with expansive glass windows and fronted by wall-size screens for tracking a rocket's progress.

Step a bit farther into the factory and there are a handful of industrial work areas separated from each other in the most informal of ways. In some spots there are blue lines on the floor and in other spots workbenches have been arranged in squares to mark off the space. It's a common sight to have one of the Merlin engines raised up in the middle of one of these work areas with a half dozen technicians wiring it up and tuning its bits and pieces.

The factory is a temple devoted to what SpaceX sees as its major weapon in the rocket-building game: in-house manufacturing. SpaceX manufactures between 80 percent and 90 percent of its rockets, engines, electronics, and other parts. It's a strategy that dumbfounds SpaceX's competitors.

A typical aerospace company comes up with the list of parts that it needs for a launch system and then hands off their design to many third parties, who then actually build the hardware. SpaceX tends to buy as little as possible to save money and because it sees depending on suppliers—especially foreign ones—as a weakness. This approach comes off as excessive at first blush. Companies have made things like radios and power distribution units for decades. Reinventing every computer and machine on a rocket could introduce more chances for error and, in general, be a waste of time.

But for SpaceX, the strategy works. In addition to building its own engines, rocket bodies, and capsules, SpaceX designs its own motherboards and circuits, sensors to detect vibrations, flight computers, and solar panels. Just by streamlining a radio, for instance, SpaceX's engineers have found that they can reduce the weight of the device by about 20 percent. And the cost savings for a home-made radio drop from between $50,000 to $100,000 for the industrial-grade equipment used by aerospace companies to $5,000 for SpaceX's unit.

It's hard to believe these price differences at first, but there are dozens if not hundreds of examples of these kinds of savings at SpaceX. The equipment at SpaceX tends to be built out of readily available consumer electronics as opposed to "space-grade" equipment used by others in the industry. SpaceX has had to work for years to convince NASA that standard electronics have gotten good enough to compete with the more expensive, specialized gear trusted in years past. To prove that it's making the right choice to NASA and itself, SpaceX will sometimes load a rocket with both the standard equipment and prototypes of its own design for testing during flight. Engineers then compare the performance characteristics of the devices. Once a SpaceX design equals or outperforms the commercial products, it becomes the chosen hardware.

Musk's growth as a CEO and rocket expert occurred alongside SpaceX's evolution as a company. At the start of the Falcon 1 journey, Musk was a forceful software executive trying to learn some basic things about a very different world. At Zip2 and PayPal, he felt comfortable standing up for his positions and directing teams of coders. At SpaceX, he had to pick things up on the job. Musk initially relied on textbooks to form the bulk of his rocketry knowledge. But as SpaceX hired one brilliant person after another, Musk realized he could tap into their stores of knowledge. He would trap an engineer in the SpaceX factory and set to work grilling him about a type of valve or specialized material.

"I thought at first that he was challenging me to see if I knew my stuff," said Kevin Brogan, one of the early engineers. "Then I realized he was trying to learn things. He would quiz you until he learned ninety percent of what you know." After a couple of years running SpaceX, Musk had turned into an aerospace expert on a level that few technology CEOs ever approach in their respective fields. "He was teaching us about the value of time, and we were teaching him about rocketry," Brogan said.

In regards to time, Musk may well set more aggressive delivery targets for very difficult-to-make products than any executive in history. Musk has been bashed by the press for setting and then missing product delivery dates. It's one of the habits that got him in the most trouble as SpaceX and Tesla tried to bring their first products to market. Time and again, Musk found himself making a public appearance where he had to come up with a new batch of excuses for a delay.

Reminded about the initial 2003 target date to fly the Falcon 1, Musk acted shocked. "Are you serious?" he said. "We said that? Okay, that's ridiculous. I think I just didn't know what the hell I was talking about. The only thing I had prior experience in was software, and, yeah, you can write a bunch of software and launch a website in a year. No problem. This isn't like software. It doesn't work that way with rockets."

Asked about his approach, Musk said that he didn't try to set impossible goals, as he thinks that is "demotivating." He also admitted that he's trying to be a bit more realistic about time frames. He added that SpaceX is not alone in setting timelines it can't meet. "Being late is par for the course in the aerospace industry," according to Musk. "It's not a question of if it's late, it's how late will the program be. I don't think an aerospace program has been completed on time since . . . World War II."

Dealing with the aggressive schedules and Musk's expectations has required SpaceX's engineers to develop a variety of survival techniques. Musk often asks for highly detailed proposals for how projects will be accomplished. The employees have learned never to break the time needed to accomplish something down into months or weeks. Musk wants day-by-day and hour-by-hour forecasts and sometimes even minute-by-minute countdowns. "You had to put in when you would go to the bathroom," Brogan said. "I'm like, 'Elon, sometimes people need to take a long dump.'"

There's no question that Musk has mastered the art of getting the most out of his employees. Interview three dozen SpaceX engineers and each one of them will have picked up on a managerial trick that Musk has used to get people to meet his deadlines. As Brogan, for example, described it: "[Musk] doesn't say, 'You have to do this by Friday at two p.m.' He says, 'I need the impossible done by Friday at two p.m. Can you do it?' Then, when you say yes, you are not working hard because he told you to. You're working hard for yourself. It's a distinction you can feel. You have signed up to do your own work."

And by hiring hundreds of bright, self-motivated people, SpaceX has maximized the power of the individual. One person putting in a sixteen-hour day ends up being much more effective than two people working eight-hour days together. The individual doesn't have to hold meetings, reach a consensus, or bring other people up to speed on a project. He just keeps working and working and working. The ideal SpaceX employee is someone like Steve Davis, the director of advanced projects at SpaceX.

"He's been working sixteen hours a day every day for years," Brogan said. "He gets more done than eleven people working together."

Davis did his tour of duty on Kwaj and considered it the greatest time of his life. "Every night, you could either sleep by the rocket in this tent shelter where the geckos crawled all over you or take this one-hour boat ride that made you seasick back to the main island," he said. "Every night, you had to pick the pain that you remembered least. You got so hot and exhausted. It was just amazing." After working on the Falcon 1, Davis moved on to the Falcon 9 and then Dragon.

The Dragon capsule took SpaceX four years to design. It's likely the fastest project of its kind done in the history of the aerospace industry. The project started with Musk and a handful of engineers, most of them under thirty years old, and peaked at one hundred people. They started by reading over every paper published by NASA and other aeronautics bodies around similar spaceships.

The engineers at SpaceX then had to advance these past efforts and bring the capsule into the modern age. Some of the areas of improvement were obvious and easily accomplished, while others required more creativity. Saturn 5 and Apollo had colossal computing bays that produced only a fraction of the computer horsepower that can be achieved today on, say, an iPad. The SpaceX engineers knew they could save a lot of room by cutting out some of the computers while also adding capabilities with their more powerful equipment. SpaceX also got the recipe for its heat shield material, called PICA, through a deal with NASA. The SpaceX engineers found out how to make the PICA material less expensively and improved the underlying technology. The total cost for Dragon came in at $300 million, which would be on the order of ten to thirty times less than capsule projects built by other companies. "The metal comes in, and we roll it out, weld it, and make things," Davis said. "We build almost everything in-house. That is why the costs have come down."

Kevin Watson can attest to that. He arrived at SpaceX in 2008 after spending twenty-four years at NASA's Jet Propulsion Laboratory. Watson worked on a wide variety of projects at JPL, including building and testing computing systems that could withstand the harsh conditions of space. JPL would typically buy expensive, specially toughened computers, and this frustrated Watson. He daydreamed about ways to handcraft much cheaper, equally effective computers. While having his job interview with Musk, Watson learned that SpaceX needed just this type of thinking. Musk wanted the bulk of a rocket's computing systems to cost no more than $10,000. It was an insane figure by aerospace industry standards, where the avionics systems for a rocket typically cost well over $10 million. "In traditional aerospace, it would cost you more than ten thousand dollars just for the food at a meeting to discuss the cost of the avionics," Watson said.

During the job interview, Watson promised Musk that he could do the improbable and deliver the $10,000 avionics system. He began working on making the computers for Dragon right after being hired. The first system was called CUCU, pronounced "cuckoo." This communications box would go inside the International Space Station and communicate back with Dragon. SpaceX produced the communication computer in record time, and it ended up as the first system of its kind to pass NASA's protocol tests on the first try. NASA officials were forced to say "cuckoo" over and over again during meetings. As the months went on, Watson and other engineers built out the complete computing systems for Dragon and then adapted the technology for Falcon 9. The avionics system ended up costing a bit more than $10,000, but it came close.

One of Watson's top discoveries at SpaceX was the test bed on the third floor of the Hawthorne factory. SpaceX has test versions of all the hardware and electronics that go into a rocket laid out on metal tables. It has, in effect, replicated the innards of a rocket end to end in order to run thousands of flight simulations. Someone "launches" the rocket from a computer and then every piece of mechanical and computing hardware is monitored with sensors. An engineer can tell a valve to open, then check to see if it opened, how quickly it opened, and the level of current running to it. This testing apparatus lets SpaceX engineers practice ahead of launches and figure out how they would deal with all manner of problems. During the actual flights, SpaceX has people in the test facility who can replicate errors seen on Falcon or Dragon and make adjustments accordingly. SpaceX has made numerous changes on the fly with this system. In one case, someone spotted an error in a software file in the hours right before a launch. SpaceX's engineers changed the file, checked how it affected the test hardware, and, when no problems were detected, sent the file to the Falcon 9, waiting on the launchpad, all in less than thirty minutes. "NASA wasn't used to this," Watson said. "If something went wrong with the shuttle, everyone was just resigned to waiting three weeks before they could try and launch again."

The guiding principle at SpaceX is to embrace your work and get stuff done. People who await guidance or detailed instructions do not do well. The same goes for workers who crave feedback. And the absolute worst thing that someone can do is inform Musk that what he's asking is impossible. "Elon will say, 'Fine. You're off the project, and I am now the CEO of the project. I will do your job and be CEO of two companies at the same time. I will deliver it,'" Brogan said. "What's crazy is that Elon actually does it. Every time he's fired someone and taken their job, he's delivered on whatever the project was."

It is jarring for both parties when the SpaceX culture rubs against more organizational bodies like NASA, the US Air Force, and the Federal Aviation Administration. One time, Musk wrote a list of things an FAA employee had said during a meeting that Musk found silly and sent the list along to the guy's boss. "And then his dingbat manager sent me this long email about how he had been in the shuttle program and in charge of twenty launches or something like that and how dare I say that the other guy was wrong," Musk said. "I told him, 'Not only is he wrong, and let me rearticulate the reasons, but you're wrong, and let me articulate the reasons.' I don't think he sent me another email after that. We're trying to have a really big impact on the space industry. If the rules are such that you can't make progress, then you have to fight the rules."

When Musk rubs outsiders the wrong way, Gwynne Shotwell is often there to try to smooth over the situation. Like Musk, she has a fiery personality, but Shotwell embraces the role of the peacemaker. These skills have allowed her to handle the day-to-day operations at SpaceX, leaving Musk to focus on the company's overall strategy, product designs, marketing, and motivating employees. Like all of Musk's most trusted lieutenants, Shotwell has been willing to stay largely in the background, do her work, and focus on the company's cause.

Shotwell grew up in the suburbs of Chicago, the daughter of an artist (mom) and a neurosurgeon (dad). She played the part of a bright, pretty girl, getting straight As at school and joining the cheerleading squad. Shotwell had not expressed a major inclination toward the sciences and knew only one version of an engineer—the guy who drives a train. But there were clues that she was wired a bit differently. She was the daughter who mowed the lawn and helped put the family basketball hoop together. In third grade, Shotwell developed a brief interest in car engines, and her mom bought a book detailing how they work. Later, in high school, Shotwell's mom forced her to attend a lecture at the Illinois Institute of Technology on a Saturday afternoon. As Shotwell listened to one of the panels, she grew enamored with a fifty-year-old mechanical engineer. "She had these beautiful clothes, this suit and shoes that I loved," Shotwell said. She chatted to the engineer after the talk, learning about her job. "That was the day I decided to become a mechanical engineer," she said.

Shotwell went on to receive an undergraduate degree in mechanical engineering and a masters degree in applied mathematics from Northwestern University. Then she took a job at Chrysler. It was a type of management training program meant for hotshot recent graduates who appeared to have leadership potential. Shotwell started out going to auto mechanic school—"I loved that"—and then from department to department. While working on engines research, Shotwell found that there were two very expensive Cray supercomputers sitting idle because none of the veterans knew how to use them. A short while later, she logged on to the computers and set them up to run computational fluid dynamics, or CFD, operations to simulate the performance of valves and other components. The work kept Shotwell interested, but the environment started to grate on her. There were rules for everything, including lots of union regulations around who could operate certain machines. "I picked up a tool once and got written up," she said. "Then I opened a bottle of liquid nitrogen and got written up. I started thinking that the job was not what I had anticipated it would be."

Shotwell pulled out of the Chrysler training program, regrouped at home, and then briefly pursued her doctorate in applied mathematics. While back on the Northwestern campus, one of her professors mentioned an opportunity at the Aerospace Corporation. Anything but a household name, Aerospace Corporation has been headquartered in El Segundo since 1960, serving as a kind of neutral, non-profit organization that advises the air force, NASA, and other federal bodies on space programs. The company has a drab feel but has proved very useful over the years with its research activities and ability to champion and nix costly endeavors. Shotwell started at Aerospace in October 1988 and worked on a wide range of projects. One job required her to develop a thermal model that depicted how temperature fluctuations in the space shuttle's cargo bay affected the performance of equipment on various payloads. She spent ten years at Aerospace and honed her skills as a systems engineer. By the end, though, Shotwell, much like Musk, had become irritated by the pace of the industry. "I didn't understand why it had to take fifteen years to make a military satellite," she said. "You could see my interest was waning."

For the next four years, Shotwell worked at Microcosm Incorporated, a space start-up just down the road from the Aerospace Corporation, and became the head of its space systems division and business development. Boasting a combination of smarts, confidence, and direct talk, Shotwell developed a reputation as a strong saleswoman. In 2002, one of her coworkers, Hans Koenigsmann, left for

SpaceX. Shotwell took Koenigsmann out for a going-away lunch and dropped him off at SpaceX's then-rinky-dink headquarters. "Hans told me to go in and meet Elon," Shotwell said. "I did, and that's when I told him, 'You need a good business development person.'" The next day, Mary Beth Brown called Shotwell and told her that Musk wanted to interview her for the new vice president of business development position. Shotwell ended up as employee number seven. "I gave three weeks' notice at Microcosm and remodeled my bathroom because I knew I would not have a life after taking the job," she said.

14

SPACEX RISING

GWYNNE SHOTWELL WAS SPACEX'S IN-HOUSE miracle worker.

Throughout the early years of the company, SpaceX did not actually have a product to sell. It took SpaceX so much longer than it had planned to have a successful flight. The failures along the way were embarrassing and bad for business. Nonetheless, Shotwell managed to sell about a dozen flights to a mix of government and commercial customers before SpaceX put its first Falcon 1 into orbit. Her deal-making skills extended to negotiating the big-ticket contracts with NASA that kept SpaceX alive during its most troubled years, including a $278 million contract in August 2006 to begin work on vehicles that could ferry supplies to the ISS. Shotwell's track record of success turned her into Musk's ultimate confidante at SpaceX, and at the end of 2008, she became president and chief operating officer at the company.

Shotwell can switch on an easygoing, likable manner and address the entire company during a meeting or convince a collection of possible recruits why they should sign up to be worked to the bone. During one such meeting with a group of interns, Shotwell pulled about a hundred people into the corner of the cafeteria. Pacing back and forth in front of the group with a microphone in hand, she asked them to announce what school they came from and what project they were working on while at SpaceX. The students were, at least by academic standards, among the most impressive youngsters in the world. They peppered Shotwell with questions. She made sure to emphasize the lean, innovative edge SpaceX has over the more traditional aerospace companies. "Our competitors are scared . . . of us," Shotwell told the group.

One of SpaceX's biggest goals, Shotwell said, was to fly as often as possible. The company has never sought to make a fortune off each flight. It would rather make a little on each launch and keep the flights flowing. A Falcon 9 flight costs $60 million. The company would like to see that figure drop to about $20 million. SpaceX spent $2.5 billion to get four Dragon capsules to the ISS, nine flights with the Falcon 9, and five flights with the Falcon 1. It's a price-per-launch total that the rest of the players in the industry cannot comprehend, let alone aspire to. "I don't know what those guys do with their money," Shotwell said.

It was while discussing SpaceX's grandest missions that Shotwell really came into her own and seemed to inspire the interns. Some of them clearly dreamed of becoming astronauts, and Shotwell said that working at SpaceX was almost certainly their best chance to get to space now that the number of astronauts at NASA had dwindled. Musk, she added, had made designing cool-looking, "non–Stay Puft" spacesuits a personal priority. "They can't be clunky and nasty," Shotwell said. "You have to do better than that." As for where the astronauts would go: well, there were space habitats (which are in the midst of being built), the moon, and, of course, Mars as options. SpaceX has already started testing a giant rocket, called the Falcon Heavy, that will take it much farther into space than the Falcon 9, and it has another, even larger spaceship on the way. "Our Falcon Heavy rocket will not take a busload of people to Mars," she said. "So there's something after Heavy. We're working on it."

To make something like that vehicle happen, she said, the SpaceX employees needed to be effective and pushy. "Make sure your output is high," Shotwell said. "If we're throwing a bunch of [garbage] in your way, you need to be mouthy about it. That's not a quality that's widely accepted elsewhere, but it is at SpaceX." And if that sounded harsh, so be it. As Shotwell saw it, the commercial space race was coming down to SpaceX and China and that's it. And in the bigger picture, the race was on to ensure man's survival. "If you hate people and think human extinction is okay, then . . . don't go to space," Shotwell said. "If you think it is worth humans doing some risk management and finding a second place to go live, then you should be focused on this issue and willing to spend some money. I am pretty sure we will be selected by NASA to drop landers and rovers off on Mars. Then the first SpaceX mission will be to drop off a bunch of supplies so that once people get there, there will be places to live and food to eat and stuff for them to do."

Outside of SpaceX, the American launch providers are no longer competitive against their peers in other countries. SpaceX's main competitor for domestic military satellites and other large payloads is United Launch Alliance (ULA), a joint venture formed in 2006 when Boeing and Lockheed Martin combined forces. The thinking at the time about the union was that the government did not have enough business for two companies and that combining the research and manufacturing work of Boeing and Lockheed would result in cheaper, safer launches. While ULA has become a model of reliability, it does not come close to competing on price against SpaceX, the Russians, or the Chinese.

To put things more bluntly, ULA has turned into something of an embarrassment for the United States. In March
2014, ULA's then-CEO, Michael Gass, faced off against
Musk during a congressional hearing that dealt, in part,
with SpaceX's request to take on more of the government's
annual launch load. A series of slides were rolled out that
showed how the government payments for launches have
skyrocketed since Boeing and Lockheed became a monop-
oly. According to Musk's math presented at the hearing,
ULA charged $380 million per flight, while SpaceX would
charge $90 million per flight. (The $90 million figure was
higher than SpaceX's standard $60 million because the
government has certain additional requirements for particularly sensitive launches.) By simply picking SpaceX as
its launch provider, Musk pointed out, the government
would save enough money to pay for the satellite going on
the rocket. Gass had no real retort.

The hearing also came as tensions between the United
States and Russia were running high due to Russia's aggressive actions in Ukraine. Musk noted that the United States
could soon be placing sanctions on Russia that could carry
over to aerospace equipment. (His prediction would prove
correct as the US did end up banning the purchase of Russian engines.) ULA, as it happens, relies on Russian-made
engines to send up sensitive US military equipment in its

Atlas V rockets. "Our Falcon 9 and Falcon Heavy launch vehicles are truly American," Musk said. "We design and manufacture our rockets in California and Texas." Gass countered that ULA had bought a two-year supply of Russian engines and purchased the blueprints to the machines and had them translated from Russian to English, and he said this with a straight face. (A few months after the hearing, ULA replaced Gass as CEO and signed a deal with Blue Origin, the rocket company founded by Amazon.com's CEO, Jeff Bezos, to develop American-made rockets.)

The government has taken notice of SpaceX's homegrown manufacturing know-how. SpaceX and Boeing, for example, won a four-year NASA competition to fly astronauts to the ISS. SpaceX will get $2.6 billion, and Boeing will get $4.2 billion to develop their capsules and ferry people to the ISS starting in 2017. The companies would, in effect, be replacing the space shuttle and restoring the United States's ability to conduct manned flights. "I actually don't mind that Boeing gets twice as much money for meeting the same NASA requirements as SpaceX with worse technology," Musk said. "Having two companies involved is better for the advancement of human space flight."

SpaceX has expanded its launch capabilities at a remarkable pace. In June 2010, the Falcon 9 flew for the first time and orbited Earth successfully. In December 2010, SpaceX proved during a test mission that the Falcon 9 could carry a Dragon capsule into space and that the capsule could be recovered safely after an ocean landing. It became the first commercial company ever to pull off this feat. Then, in May 2012, SpaceX went through the most significant moment in the company's history since that first successful launch on Kwajalein.

On May 22, at 3:44 a.m., a Falcon 9 rocket took off from the Kennedy Space Center in Florida. The rocket boosted Dragon into space and then let the capsule go off on its own. Its solar panels fanned out and the capsule fired up its eighteen Draco thrusters, or small rocket engines, to guide its path to the International Space Station. The SpaceX engineers worked in shifts—some of them sleeping on cots at the factory—as it took the capsule three days to make its journey. They spent most of the time watching Dragon's flight and checking to see that its sensor systems were picking up the ISS. Originally, Dragon planned to dock with the ISS around four a.m. on the twenty-fifth, but as the capsule approached the space station, an unexpected glint of light kept throwing off the calculations of a laser used to measure the distance between Dragon and the ISS. "I remember it being two and a half hours of struggle," Shotwell said. Fearing all the time that the mission would be aborted, SpaceX decided to upload some new software to Dragon that would

cut the size of the visual frame used by the sensors to elim-
inate the effect of the sunlight on the machine. Then, just
before seven a.m., Dragon got close enough to the ISS for
Don Pettit, an astronaut, to use a fifty-eight-foot robotic arm
to reach out and grab the resupply capsule.

About thirty people were in the control room when the
docking happened. Over the next couple of hours, workers
streamed into the SpaceX factory to soak up the joy and
excitement of the moment. SpaceX had set another first, as
the only private company to dock with the ISS. A couple of
months later, SpaceX received $440 million from NASA to
keep developing Dragon so that it could transport people.

*With a Dragon capsule hanging overhead, SpaceX employees peer into the company's mission
control center at the Hawthorne factory. Photograph courtesy of SpaceX*

In May 2014, Musk invited the press to SpaceX's head-quarters to demonstrate what some of that NASA money had bought. He unveiled the Dragon V2, or version two, spacecraft. People arrived in Hawthorne by the hundreds and watched as Musk popped open the capsule's door with a bump of his fist. What he revealed was spectacular. The cramped quarters of past capsules were gone. There were seven thin, sturdy seats arranged with four seats close to the main console and a row of three seats in the back. Musk walked around in the capsule to show how roomy it was and then plopped down in the central captain's chair. He reached up and unlocked a flat-screen console that gracefully slid down right in front of the first row of seats. Someone had finally built a spaceship worthy of scientist and moviemaker dreams.

There was substance to go with the style. Dragon 2 will be able to dock with the ISS and other space habitats auto-matically without needing the intervention of a robotic arm. It will run on a SuperDraco engine—a thruster made by SpaceX and the first engine ever built completely by a 3-D printer to go into space. This means that a machine formed the engine out of a single piece of metal so that its strength and performance should exceed anything built by humans welding various parts together. And most mind-boggling of all, Musk revealed that Dragon 2 will be able to land anywhere on Earth that SpaceX wants by using the SuperDraco engines and thrusters to come to a gentle stop on the ground. No more landings at sea. No more throwing spaceships away. "That is how a twenty-first-century spaceship should land," Musk said. "You can just reload propellant and fly again. So long as we continue to throw away rockets and spacecraft, we will never have true access to space."

In 2014, Musk unveiled a radical new take on the space capsule—Dragon V2. It comes with a drop-down touch screen display and slick interior. Photograph courtesy of SpaceX

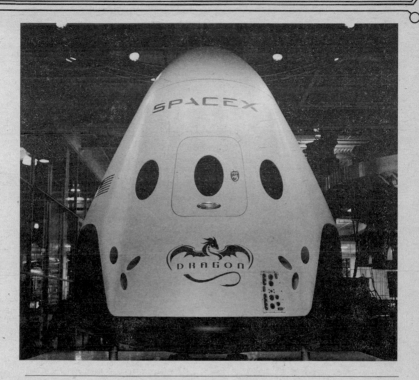

Dragon V2 will be able to return to Earth and land with pinpoint accuracy. Photograph courtesy of SpaceX

Dragon 2 is just one of the machines that SpaceX continues to develop in parallel. One of the company's next milestones will be the first flight of the Falcon Heavy, which is designed to be the world's most powerful rocket. SpaceX has found a way to combine three Falcon 9s into a single craft with twenty-seven of the Merlin engines and the ability to carry more than fifty-three metric tons of stuff into orbit. Part of the genius of Musk and Mueller's designs is that SpaceX can reuse the same engine in different configurations—from the Falcon 1 up to the Falcon Heavy—saving on cost and time. SpaceX is also busy building a spaceport from the ground up. The goal is to be able to launch many rockets from this facility located in Brownsville, Texas, by automating the processes needed to stand a rocket up on the pad, fuel it, and send it off.

The lingering question for many SpaceX employees is when exactly they will see a big reward for all their work. SpaceX's staff is paid well but by no means exceptionally. Many of them expect to make their money when SpaceX files for an initial public offering, or IPO, on the stock market. At that point, anyone is free to invest in the company, and the thinking is that the value of SpaceX would rise a lot as outsiders pour money into it. The employees could then sell their shares in SpaceX whenever they want and profit from the sales.

The thing is that Musk does not want to sell shares to the public any time soon, and understandably so. It's a bit hard to explain the whole Mars thing to investors, when it's unclear what the business model around starting a colony on another planet will be. When the employees heard Musk say during a meeting that an IPO was years away and would not occur until the Mars mission looked more secure, they started to complain. After Musk found out about the gripes, he addressed all of SpaceX in an email. In it, he said, "I am increasingly concerned about SpaceX going public before the Mars transport system is in place. Creating the technology needed to establish life on Mars is and always has been the fundamental goal of SpaceX. If being a public company diminishes that likelihood, then we should not do so until Mars is secure."

15

THE REVENGE OF THE ELECTRIC CAR

IN THE MIDDLE OF 2012, Tesla Motors stunned its rival carmakers when it began shipping the Model S sedan. This all-electric luxury vehicle could go more than three hundred miles on a single charge. It could reach sixty miles per hour in 4.2 seconds. It could seat seven people, if you used a couple of rear-facing child seats in the back. It also had two trunks. There was the standard one and then what Tesla calls a "frunk" up front, where a bulky gas-burning engine would usually be. The Model S ran on an electric battery pack that makes up the base of the car and a watermelon-size electric motor located between the rear tires. Getting rid of the engine and its din of clanging machinery also meant that the Model

S ran silently. Tesla's car outclassed most other luxury sedans in terms of raw speed, mileage, handling, and storage space.

The Tesla Model S sedan with its electric motor (near the rear) and battery pack (bottom) exposed. Photograph courtesy of Tesla Motors

And there was more—like the cutesy thing with the door handles, which were flush with the car's body until the driver got close to the Model S. Then the silver handles would pop out, the driver would open the door and get in, and the handles would retract even with the car's body again. Once inside, the driver encountered a seventeen-inch touch screen that controlled the majority of the car's functions, be it raising the volume on the stereo or opening the sunroof with a slide of the finger. Whereas most cars have large dashboards to accommodate various displays and buttons and to protect people from the noise of the engine, the Model S offered up vast amounts of space. The Model S had an ever-present internet connection, allowing the driver to stream music through the touch console and to display massive Google maps for navigation. The driver didn't need to turn a key or even push an ignition button to start the car. His weight in the seat coupled with a sensor in the keychain was enough to activate the vehicle. Made of lightweight aluminum, the car achieved the highest safety rating in history. And it could be recharged *for free* at Tesla's charging stations lining highways across the United States and later around the world.

For both engineers and green-minded people, the Model S presented a model of efficiency. Traditional cars and hybrids have anywhere from hundreds to thousands of moving parts. An internal combustion engine must perform constant, controlled explosions with pistons, crank-shafts, oil filters, alternators, fans, distributors, valves, coils, and cylinders among the many pieces of machinery needed for the work. The oomph produced by the engine must then be passed through clutches, gears, and driveshafts to make the wheels turn, and then exhaust systems have to deal with the waste.

It turns out then that cars are not very good at taking gasoline, burning it, and translating that burst of energy into movement. Only about 10–20 percent of the gaso-line ends up being used to push the car forward. Most of the energy (about 70 percent) is lost as heat in the engine, while the rest is lost through wind resistance, braking, and other mechanical functions. The Model S, by contrast, has about a dozen moving parts, with the battery pack sending energy instantly to the small motor that turns the wheels. The Model S ends up being about 60 percent efficient, losing most of the rest of its energy to heat. The sedan gets the equivalent of 100 miles per gallon.

Yet another distinguishing characteristic of the Model S was the experience of buying and owning the car. You didn't go to a dealership and argue with a pushy salesman. Tesla sold the Model S directly through its own stores and website. Typically, the stores were placed in high-end malls or affluent suburbs, not far from the Apple stores on which they were modeled. Customers would walk in and find a Model S in the middle of the shop and often an exposed version of the car's base near the back of the store to show off the battery pack and motor. There were massive touch screens where people could calculate how much they might save on fuel costs by moving to an all-electric car and where they could configure the add-ons for their future Model S. Once the configuration process was done, the customer could give the screen a big swipe and his Model S would theatrically appear on an even bigger screen in the center of the store. If you wanted to sit in the display model, a salesperson would pull back a red velvet rope near the driver's-side door and let you enter the car. The salespeople were not compensated on commission, or what they sold, and didn't have to try to talk you into buying a bunch of extra features.

Whether you bought the car in the store or online, Tesla would deliver it to your home, office, or anywhere else you wanted. The company also offered customers the option of picking their cars up from the factory in Silicon Valley and treating their friends and family to a complimentary tour of the facility. In the months that followed the delivery, there were no oil changes or tune-ups to be dealt with because the Model S didn't need them. It had done away with so much of the mechanical dreck standard in an internal combustion vehicle. However, if something did go wrong with the car, Tesla would come pick it up and give the customer a loaner while it repaired the Model S.

The Model S also offered to fix problems in a new way for a mass-produced car. Some of the early owners complained about glitches like the door handles not popping out quite right or their windshield wipers operating at funky speeds. These were inexcusable flaws for such a costly vehicle, but Tesla addressed them with clever efficiency. While the owners slept, Tesla's engineers tapped into the cars via the internet connection and downloaded software updates. When a customer took the car out for a spin in the morning and found it working right, he was left feeling as if magical elves had done the work.

Tesla soon began showing off its software skills for jobs other than fixing mistakes. It put out a smartphone app that let people turn on their air-conditioning or heating from afar and see where the car was parked on a map. Tesla also began installing software updates that gave the Model S new features. Overnight, the Model S could suddenly recharge much faster than before or possessed a new range of voice controls. Tesla had transformed the car into a gadget—a device that actually got better after you bought it. As Craig Venter, one of the earliest Model S owners and the famed scientist who first decoded man's DNA, put it, "It changes everything about transportation. It's a computer on wheels."

The first people to notice what Tesla had accomplished were the geeks in Silicon Valley. The region is filled with early adopters willing to buy the latest gizmos and suffer through their imperfections. Normally, this habit applies to computing devices ranging from $100 to $2,000 in price. This time around, the early adopters were willing not only to spend $100,000 on a product that might not work but also to trust their physical well-being to a start-up. Tesla needed this early boost of confidence and got it on a scale few expected. In the first couple of months after the Model S went on sale, you might see one or two Model S vehicles per day on the streets of San Francisco and the surrounding cities. Then you started to see five to ten per day. Soon enough, the Model S seemed to feel like the most common car in the heart of Silicon Valley. The Model S emerged as the ultimate status symbol for wealthy technophiles, allowing them to show off, get a new gadget and claim to be helping the environment at the same time. From Silicon Valley, the Model S phenomenon spread to Los Angeles, then all along the West Coast and then, to a lesser extent, to Washington, DC, and New York.

At first the other automakers viewed the Model S as a gimmick and its surging sales as part of a fad. These thoughts soon gave way to something closer to panic. In November 2012, just a few months after it started shipping, the Model S was named *Motor Trend*'s Car of the Year in the first unanimous vote that anyone at the magazine could remember. The Model S beat out eleven other vehicles from companies such as Porsche, BMW, Lexus, and Subaru and was heralded as "proof positive that America can still make great things." Several months later, *Consumer Reports* gave the Model S its highest car rating in history—99 out of 100—while proclaiming that it was likely the best car ever built. It was at about this time that sales of the Model S started to soar and General Motors, among other automakers, pulled together a team to study the Model S, Tesla, and the methods of Elon Musk.

Tesla began shipping the Model S sedan in 2012. The car ended up winning most of the automotive industry's major awards. Photograph courtesy of Tesla Motors

It's worth pausing for a moment to think about what Tesla had accomplished since 2008. Musk had set out to make an electric car without compromises. He did that. Then he upended the decades of criticisms against electric cars. The Model S was not just the best electric car; it was the best car, period, and *the* car people desired. America had not seen a successful car company since Chrysler emerged in 1925. Silicon Valley had done little in the automotive industry, and Musk had never run a car factory before. Yet, one year after the Model S went on sale, Tesla had started to make money on every car it sold and was selling $562 million worth of cars every three months. This young, tiny company had become as valuable as Mazda Motor, one of Japan's best known and largest automakers. Elon Musk had built the automotive equivalent of the iPhone.

You can forgive the automotive industry veterans for being caught unawares. For years, Tesla had looked like an utter disaster incapable of doing much of anything right.

It took until early 2009 for Tesla to really hit its stride with the Roadster and work out the manufacturing issues behind the sports car. Then, just as the company tried to build some momentum around the Roadster, Tesla stumbled again. Musk sent out an email to customers declaring a price hike. Where the car originally started around $92,000, it would now start at $109,000. In the email, Musk said that four hundred customers who had already placed their orders for a Roadster but not yet received them would bear the brunt of the price change and need to cough up the extra cash.

He argued that the company had had no choice but to raise prices. The manufacturing costs for the Roadster had come in much higher than the company initially expected, and Tesla needed to prove that it could make the cars at a profit to improve its chances of securing a large government loan. Tesla needed that loan in order to build a factory to produce the Model S. "I firmly believe that the plan . . . strikes a reasonable compromise between being fair to early customers and ensuring the viability of Tesla, which is obviously in the best interests of all customers," Musk wrote in the email. "Mass-market electric cars have been my goal from the beginning of Tesla. I don't want and I don't think the vast majority of Tesla customers want us to do anything to jeopardize that objective." While some Tesla customers grumbled, Musk had largely read his customer base right. They would support just about anything he suggested.

Following the price increase, Tesla had a safety recall. It said that Lotus, the manufacturer of the Roadster's chassis, had failed to tighten a bolt properly on its assembly line. On the plus side, Tesla had only delivered about 345 Roadsters, which meant that it could fix the problem in a manageable fashion. On the downside, a safety recall was the last thing a car start-up needed. The next year, Tesla had another voluntary recall. It had received a report of a power cable grinding against the body of the Roadster to the point that it caused a short circuit and some smoke. That time, Tesla brought 439 Roadsters in for a fix. Tesla did its best to put a positive spin on these issues, saying that it would make "house calls" to fix the Roadsters or pick up the cars and take them back to the factory. Ever since, Musk has tried to turn any problem with a Tesla into an excuse to show off the company's attention to service and dedication to pleasing the customer. More often than not, the strategy has worked.

Tesla did just enough to survive. From 2008 to 2012, Tesla sold about 2,500 Roadsters. The car had accomplished what Musk had intended from the outset. It proved that electric cars could be fun to drive and that they could be objects of desire.

As difficult as creating the Roadster had been, the adventure had made Musk excited to see what vehicle Tesla could produce starting with a clean slate. Tesla's next car—code-named WhiteStar—would not be a modified version of another company's vehicle. It would be made from scratch and structured to take full advantage of what the electric car technology offered. The battery pack in the Roadster, for example, had to be placed near the rear of the car to fit within the Lotus Elise chassis. This was okay but not ideal due to the weight of the batteries. With WhiteStar, which would become the Model S, Musk and Tesla's engineers knew from the start that they would place the 1,300-pound battery pack on the base of the car. This would give the vehicle a low center of gravity and excellent handling.

The mechanics of the car, though, were just part of what would make the Model S shine. Musk wanted to make a statement with the car's look as well. It would be a sedan, yes, but it would be an exciting sedan. It would also be comfortable and luxurious and have none of the compromises that Tesla had been forced to embrace with the Roadster.

A large car company might spend $1 billion and need thousands of people to design a new vehicle and bring it to market. Tesla had nothing close to these resources as it gave birth to the Model S. According to Ron Lloyd, the former vice president of the WhiteStar project, Tesla initially aimed to make about ten thousand Model S sedans per year and had budgeted around $130 million to achieve this goal, including engineering the car and acquiring the manufacturing machines needed to stamp out the body parts. "One of the things Elon pushed hard with everyone was to do as much as possible in-house," Lloyd said. Tesla would make up for its lack of R&D money by hiring smart people who could outwork and outthink the other companies relied on by the rest of the automakers. "The mantra was that one great engineer will replace three medium ones," Lloyd said.

A small team of Tesla engineers purchased a Mercedes CLS four-door coupe as a type of experimental model for their future sedan. They brought the car to Tesla's research facility in Silicon Valley and tore it apart. Tesla's engineers cut the floor out of the CLS and then slid in one of their flat battery packs. Next, they put the electronics that tied the whole system together in the trunk. After that, they replaced the interior of the car to restore its fit and finish. Following three months of work, Tesla had in effect built an all-electric Mercedes CLS.

Tesla used the car to impress investors and future partners like Daimler, a famous German car company that
makes cars under the Mercedes brand along with many
others, which would eventually turn to Tesla for electric
powertrains in their vehicles. Now and again, the Tesla team
took the car out for drives on public roads. It weighed more
than the Roadster but was still fast and had a range of about
120 miles per charge. To drive around in relative secrecy, the
engineers would weld the tips of the exhaust pipes back onto
the car to make it look like any other CLS.

It was at this time, the summer of 2008, when an artsy
car lover named Franz von Holzhausen joined Tesla. His
job would be to oversee the transition from the prototype
vehicle to Tesla's original sedan design.

Von Holzhausen grew up thinking about and drawing
cars. After graduating in 1992 from the Art Center College
of Design in Los Angeles, he started work for Volkswagen on
just about the most exciting project imaginable—a top secret
new version of the Beetle. "It really was a magical time," von
Holzhausen said. "Only fifty people in the world knew we
were doing this project." In 1997, Volkswagen launched the
"New Beetle," and von Holzhausen saw firsthand how the
look of the car captivated the public and changed the way
people felt about Volkswagen. "It started a rebirth of the VW
brand and brought design back into their mix," he said.

Von Holzhausen spent eight years with VW, climbing the ranks of its design team and falling in love with the car culture of Southern California. Los Angeles has long adored its cars, and almost all of the major carmakers set up design studios in the city. The presence of the studios allowed von Holzhausen eventually to hop from VW to General Motors and Mazda, where he served as the company's director of design.

When Musk met the free-spirited, creative von Holzhausen, he immediately went to work persuading von Holzhausen to join Tesla. They took a tour of the SpaceX factory in Hawthorne and Tesla's headquarters in Silicon Valley. Both facilities were chaotic and reeked of start-up chaos. Musk ramped up the charm and sold von Holzhausen on the idea that he had a chance to shape the future of the automobile and that it made sense to leave his cushy job at a big, proven automaker for this once-in-a-lifetime opportunity.

"Elon and I went for a drive in the Roadster, and everyone was checking it out," von Holzhausen said. "I knew I could stay at Mazda for ten years and get very comfortable or take a huge leap of faith. At Tesla, there was no history, no baggage. There was just a vision of products that could change the world. Who wouldn't want to be involved with that?"

While von Holzhausen knew the risks of going to a

start-up, he could not have realized just how close Tesla was to bankruptcy when he joined the company in August 2008. Musk had coaxed von Holzhausen away from a secure job and into the jaws of death. But in many ways, this was what von Holzhausen sought at that point in his career. Tesla did not feel as much like a car company as a bunch of guys in pursuit of a very big idea. "To me, it was exciting," he said. "It was like a garage experiment, and it made cars cool again." The suits were gone, and in their stead, von Holzhausen found energetic geeks who didn't realize that what they wanted to do was borderline impossible. Musk's presence added to the energy and gave von Holzhausen confidence that Tesla actually could outflank much, much larger competitors. "Elon's mind was always way beyond the present moment," he said. "You could see that he was a step or three ahead of everyone else and one hundred percent committed to what we were doing."

Once von Holzhausen agreed to join Tesla, the company set to work quickly trying to bring his vision for the Model S to life. In a bid to save money, Musk set up the first Tesla design studio inside of the SpaceX factory. A handful of people on von Holzhausen's team took over one corner and put up a tent to add some separation and secrecy to what they were doing. In the tradition of many a Musk employee, von Holzhausen had to set up his own office.

He made a pilgrimage to IKEA to buy some desks and then went to an art store to get some paper and pens.

As von Holzhausen began sketching the outside of the Model S, the Tesla engineers had started up a project to build another electric CLS. They ripped this one down to its very core, removing all of the body structure and then stretching the wheelbase by four inches to match up with some of the early Model S specifications. Things began moving fast for everyone involved in the Model S project. In the span of about three months, von Holzhausen had designed 95 percent of what people see today with the Model S, and the engineers had started building a prototype exterior around the skeleton.

Musk hired Franz von Holzhausen in 2008 to design the Tesla Model S. The two men speak almost every day, as can be seen in this meeting in Musk's SpaceX cubicle. © Steve Jurvetson

Throughout this process, von Holzhausen and Musk talked every day. Their desks were close, and the men had a natural rapport. Musk said he wanted a style that borrowed from Aston Martin and Porsche and some specific functions. He insisted, for example, that the car seat seven people. Von Holzhausen would wonder how they would make that happen in a sedan, but he also understood where Musk was coming from. "[Musk] had five kids and wanted something that could be thought of as a family vehicle, and he knew other people would have this issue," von Holzhausen said.

Musk wanted to make another statement with a huge touch screen. This was years before the iPad would be released. The touch screens that people ran into now and again at airports or shopping kiosks were for the most part terrible. But to Musk, the iPhone and all of its touch functions made it obvious that this type of technology would soon become commonplace. He would make the equivalent of a giant iPhone and have it handle most of the car's functions. To find the right size for the screen, Musk and von Holzhausen would sit in the skeleton car and hold up laptops of different sizes, placing them horizontally and vertically to see what looked best. They settled on a seventeen-inch screen in a vertical position. Drivers would tap on this screen for every task except for opening the glove box and turning on the emergency lights—jobs required by law to be performed with physical buttons.

Since the battery pack at the base of the car would weigh so much, Musk, the designers, and the engineers were always looking for ways to reduce the Model S's weight in other spots. Musk opted to solve a big chunk of this problem by making the body of the Model S out of light-weight aluminum instead of steel. "The non-battery-pack portion of the car has to be lighter than comparable gaso-line cars, and making it all aluminum became the obvious decision," Musk said.

The huge problem with this choice was that car man-ufacturers in North America at the time had almost no experience producing aluminum body panels. Aluminum tends to tear when worked by large metal presses. It also develops lines that look like stretch marks on skin and make it difficult to lay down smooth coats of paint.

Inside of Tesla, attempts were repeatedly made to talk Musk out of the aluminum body, but he would not budge, seeing it as the only rational choice. It would be up to the Tesla team to figure out how to make the aluminum manu-facturing happen. "We knew it could be done," Musk said. "It was a question of how hard it would be and how long it would take us to sort it out."

Just about all of the major design choices with the

Model S came with similar challenges. "When we first talked about the touch screen, the guys came back and said, 'There's nothing like that in the automotive supply chain,'" Musk said. "I said, 'I know. That's because it's never been put in a . . . car before.'" Musk figured that computer manufacturers had tons of experience making seventeen-inch laptop screens, and expected them to knock out a screen for the Model S with relative ease. "The laptops are pretty robust," Musk said. "You can drop them and leave them out in the sun, and they still have to work."

After contacting the laptop suppliers, Tesla's engineers came back and said that the temperature and vibration loads for the computers did not appear to be up to auto-motive standards. As Musk dug into the situation more, he discovered that the laptop screens simply had not been tested before under the tougher automotive conditions, which included large temperature fluctuations. When Tesla performed the tests, the electronics ended up functioning just fine. Tesla also started working hand in hand with the Asian manufacturers to perfect their touch technology. "I'm pretty sure that we ended up with the only seventeen-inch touch screen in the world," Musk said. "None of the computer makers or Apple had made it work yet."

To crank up the pace of the Model S design, there were engineers working all day and then others who would show up at nine p.m. and work through the night. Both groups huddled inside of the three-thousand-square-foot tent placed on the SpaceX factory floor. "The SpaceX guys were amazingly respectful and didn't peek or ask questions," said Ali Javidan, one of the main engineers. As von Holzhausen delivered his specifications, the engineers built the prototype body of the car. Every Friday afternoon, they brought what they had made into a courtyard behind the factory, where Musk would look it over and provide feedback. To run tests on the body, the car would be loaded up with weights to represent five people and then do loops around the factory until it overheated or broke down.

The more von Holzhausen learned about Tesla's financial struggles, the more he wanted the public to see the Model S. "Things were so precarious, and I didn't want to miss our opportunity to get this thing finished and show it to the world," he said. That moment came in March 2009, when, just six months after von Holzhausen had arrived, Tesla unveiled the Model S at a press event held at SpaceX.

Amid rocket engines and hunks of aluminum, Tesla showed off a gray Model S sedan. From a distance, the display model looked glamorous and refined. The media reports from the day described the car as a mix of an Aston Martin and a Maserati. In reality, the sedan barely held together. It still had the base structure of a Mercedes CLS, although no one in the press knew that, and some of the body panels and the hood were stuck to the frame with magnets. "They could just slide the hood right off," said Bruce Leak, a Tesla owner invited to attend the event. "It wasn't really attached."

A couple of the Tesla engineers practiced test-driving the car for a couple of days leading up to the event to make sure that they knew just how long the car would go before it overheated. While not perfect, the display accomplished exactly what Musk had intended. It reminded people that Tesla had a credible plan to make electric cars more mainstream and that its cars were far more ambitious than what big-time automakers like GM and Nissan seemed to have in mind both from a design and a range perspective.

The messy reality, though, was that the odds of Tesla advancing the Model S from a prop to a sellable car were tiny. The company had the know-how for the job. It just didn't have much money or a factory that could crank out cars by the thousands. Building an entire car would require blanking machines that take sheets of aluminum and chop them up into the appropriate size for doors, hoods, and body panels. Next up would be the massive stamping machines and metal dies used to take the aluminum and bend it into precise shapes. Then there would be dozens of robots that would aid in assembling the cars, computer-controlled milling machines for precise metalwork, painting equipment, and a number of other machines for running tests. It was an investment that would run into the hundreds of millions of dollars. Musk would also need to hire thousands of workers.

Musk has long had a thing for robots and is always evaluating new machines for both the SpaceX and Tesla factories. © Steve Jurvetson

As with SpaceX, Musk preferred to build as much of Tesla's vehicles in-house as possible, but the high costs were limiting just how much Tesla could take on itself. "The original plan was that we would do final assembly," said Diarmuid O'Connell, the vice president of business development at Tesla. Partners would stamp out the body parts, do the welding and handle the painting, and ship everything to Tesla, where workers would turn the parts into a whole car. Tesla proposed to build a factory to handle this type of work first in Albuquerque, New Mexico, and then later in San Jose, California, and then pulled back on these proposals, much to the dismay of city officials in both locales. The public hemming and hawing around picking the factory site did little to inspire confidence in Tesla's ability to knock out a second car.

O'Connell joined Tesla in 2006 to help solve some of the factory and financing issues. He had been doing management consulting work in 2001 when the planes hit the Twin Towers in New York City on September 11. In the wake of the terrorist attacks, O'Connell decided to serve the United States in any way that he could. In his late thirties, he had missed the window to be a soldier and instead focused his attention on trying to get into national security work. O'Connell went from office to office in Washington, DC, looking for a job and had little luck until Lincoln Bloomfield, the assistant secretary of state for political-military affairs, heard him out. Bloomfield needed someone who could help prioritize military missions in the Middle East and make sure the right people were working on the right things, and he figured that O'Connell's management consulting experience made him a nice fit for the job. O'Connell became Bloomfield's chief of staff and dealt with a wide range of charged situations, from trade negotiations to setting up an embassy in Baghdad. After gaining security clearance, O'Connell also had access to a daily report that collected information from intelligence and military personnel on the status of operations in Iraq and Afghanistan. "Every morning at six a.m., the first thing to hit my desk was this overnight report that included information on who got killed and what killed them," O'Connell said. "I kept thinking, 'This is insane. Why are we in this place?' It was not just Iraq but the whole picture. Why were we so invested in that part of the world?" The unsurprising answer that O'Connell came up with was oil.

O'Connell decided that the rational thing to do for his country and for his newborn son was to help make the United States less dependent on oil. He looked at the wind industry and the solar industry but was unimpressed with their prospects. Then, while reading *Businessweek* magazine, he stumbled on an article about a start-up called Tesla Motors and went to the company's website, which described Tesla as a place "where we are doing things, not talking about things." "I sent an email telling them I had come from the national security area and was really passionate about reducing our dependence on oil and figured it was just a dead-letter type of thing," O'Connell said. "I got an email back the next day."

Musk hired O'Connell and quickly dispatched him to Washington, DC, to start poking around on what types of tax credits and rebates Tesla might be able to drum up for its electric vehicles. At the same time, O'Connell drafted an application for a Department of Energy stimulus package that might supply it with some much-needed cash. Tesla sought between $100 million and $200 million, grossly underestimating what it would ultimately take to build the Model S. "We were naïve and learning our way in the business," O'Connell said.

At a trade show in January 2009, Tesla attracted the attention of the big boys. Not long after the show, Daimler voiced some interest in seeing what an electric Mercedes A-Class car might look like. Daimler executives said they would visit Tesla in about a month to discuss this proposition in detail, and the Tesla engineers decided to blow them away by producing two prototype vehicles before the visit. When the Daimler executives saw what Tesla had done, they ordered four thousand of Tesla's battery packs for a fleet of test vehicles in Germany. The Tesla team pulled off the same kind of feats for Toyota and won its business too.

In May 2009, things started to take off for Tesla. The Model S had been unveiled, and Daimler followed that by acquiring a 10 percent stake in Tesla for $50 million. The companies also formed a strategic partnership to have Tesla provide the battery packs for one thousand of Daimler's smart cars. "That money was important and went a long way back then," said O'Connell. "It was also a validation. Here is the company that invented the internal combustion engine, and they are investing in us. It was a seminal moment, and I am sure it gave the guys over at the Department of Energy the feeling that we were real. It's not just our scientists saying this stuff is good. It's Mercedes freaking Benz."

Sure enough, in January 2010, the Department of Energy struck a $465 million loan agreement with Tesla. The money was far more than Tesla had ever expected to get from the government. But it still represented just a fraction of the $1 billion plus that most carmakers needed to bring a new vehicle to market. So, while Musk and O'Connell were thrilled to get the money, they still wondered if Tesla would be able to live up to the bargain. Tesla would need one more lucky break or, perhaps, to steal a car factory. And in May 2010, that's more or less what it did.

16

TESLA'S IPHONE MOMENT

GENERAL MOTORS AND TOYOTA HAD teamed up in 1984 to build New United Motor Manufacturing Inc., or NUMMI, on the site of a former GM assembly plant in Fremont, California, a city on the outskirts of Silicon Valley. The companies hoped the joint facility would combine the best of American and Japanese auto-making skills and result in higher quality, cheaper cars. The factory went on to pump out millions of vehicles. Then the recession of 2008 hit, and GM found itself trying to climb out of bankruptcy. It decided to abandon the plant in 2009, and Toyota followed right after, saying it would close down the whole facility, leaving five thousand people without jobs.

All of a sudden, Tesla had the chance to buy a 5.3-million-square-foot plant in its backyard. Just one month after the last Toyota Corolla went off the manufacturing line in April 2010, Tesla and Toyota announced a partnership and transfer of the factory. Tesla agreed to pay $42 million for a large portion of the factory (once worth $1 billion), while Toyota invested $50 million in Tesla for a 2.5 percent stake in the company. Tesla had basically secured a factory, including the massive metal-stamping machines and other equipment, for free.

Tesla took over the New United Motor Manufacturing Inc. (or NUMMI) car factory in Fremont, California, which is where workers produce the Model S sedan. Photograph courtesy of SpaceX

The string of fortunate turns for Tesla left Musk feeling good. Just after the factory deal closed in the summer of 2010, Tesla started the process of filing for an initial public offering. The company obviously needed as much money as it could get to bring the Model S to market and push forward with its other technology projects. Tesla hoped to raise about $200 million.

For Musk, going public represented something of a deal with the devil. Ever since the Zip2 and PayPal days, Musk has done everything in his power to maintain absolute control over his companies. Even if he remained the largest shareholder in Tesla, the company would be subjected to the unreliable and capricious nature of the public markets. Musk, the ultimate long-term thinker, would face constant second-guessing from investors looking for short-term returns. Tesla would also be subject to public scrutiny, as it would be forced to open its financial books for all to review. This was bad because Musk prefers to operate in secrecy and because Tesla's financial situation looked awful. The company had one product (the Roadster), had huge development costs, and had bordered on bankruptcy months earlier.

Tesla went public on June 29, 2010. It raised $226 million, with the company's shares shooting up 41 percent that day. Investors looked past Tesla's $55.7 million loss in 2009 and the more than $300 million the company had spent in seven years and bought into its vision. The IPO stood as the first for an American carmaker since Ford went public in 1956.

Flush with funds, Musk began expanding some of the engineering teams. Tesla's main offices moved from San Mateo to a larger building in Palo Alto, and von Holzhausen expanded the design team in Los Angeles. Javidan hopped between projects, helping develop technology for the electrified Mercedes-Benz, an electric Toyota RAV4, and prototypes of the Model S. The Tesla team worked fast inside of a tiny lab with about forty-five people knocking out thirty-five RAV4 test vehicles at the rate of about two cars per week. The alpha—or early test—version of the Model S, including newly stamped body parts from the Fremont factory, a revamped battery pack, and revamped power electronics, came to life in the basement of the Palo Alto office. "The first prototype was finished at about two a.m.," Javidan said. "We were so excited that we drove it around without glass, any interior, or a hood."

A day or two later, Musk came to check out the vehicle. He jumped into the car and drove it to the opposite end of the basement, where he could spend some time alone with it. He got out and walked around the vehicle, and then the engineers came over to hear his take on the machine. This process would be repeated many times in the months to come. "He would generally be positive but constructive," Javidan said. "We would try and get him rides whenever we could, and he might ask for the steering to be tighter or something like that before running off to another meeting."

Like the employees at SpaceX, Tesla employees developed techniques for dealing with Musk's high demands. The savvy engineers knew better than to go into a meeting and deliver bad news without some sort of alternative plan at the ready. "One of the scariest meetings was when we needed to ask Elon for an extra two weeks and more money to build out another version of the Model S," Javidan said. "We put together a plan, stating how long things would take and what they would cost. We told him that if he wanted the car in thirty days it would require hiring some new people, and we presented him with a stack of résumés. You don't tell Elon you can't do something. That will get you kicked out of the room. You need everything lined up." Other employees were surprised that Javidan survived that meeting without getting fired, but after he presented Musk with the plan, Musk just said, "Okay, thanks."

There were times when Musk would overwhelm the Tesla engineers with his requests. He took a Model S prototype home for a weekend and came back on Monday asking for around eighty changes. Since Musk never writes anything down, he held all the alterations in his head, and would run down the checklist week by week to see what the engineers had fixed. The same engineering rules as those at SpaceX applied. You did what Musk asked or were prepared to thoroughly explain why something could not be done.

As the development of the Model S neared completion in 2012, Musk went over the Model S with von Holzhausen every Friday at Tesla's design studio in Los Angeles. Von Holzhausen and his small team had moved out of the corner in the SpaceX factory and gotten their own hangar-shaped facility near the rear of the SpaceX complex. The building had a few offices and then one large, wide-open area where various mock-ups of vehicles and parts awaited inspection.

Finally, on June 22, 2012, Tesla invited all of its employees, some select customers, and the press to its factory in Fremont to watch as the first Model S sedans were taken home. Depending on which of the many promised delivery dates you pick, the Model S was anywhere from eighteen months to two-plus years late. Some of the delays were a result of Musk's requests for exotic technologies that needed to be invented. Other delays were simply a function of this still-quite-young automaker learning how to produce an immaculate luxury vehicle and needing to go through the trial and error tied to becoming a more mature company.

The Model S launch event took place in a section of the factory where they finish off the cars. There's a part of the floor with various grooves and bumps that the cars pass over as technicians listen for any rattles. There's also a chamber where water can be sprayed at high pressure onto the car to check for leaks. For the very last inspection, the Model S cruises onto a raised platform made out of bamboo, which, when coupled with lots of LED lighting, is meant to provide an abundant amount of contrast so that people can spot flaws on the body. For the first few months that the Model S came off the line, Musk went to this bamboo stage to inspect every vehicle. "He was down on all fours looking up under the wheel well," said Steve Jurvetson, investor and Tesla board member.

Hundreds of people had gathered around this stage to watch as the first dozen or so cars were presented to their owners. Many of the employees were factory workers who had once been part of the autoworkers' union, lost their jobs when the NUMMI plant closed, and were now back at work again, making the car of the future. They waved American flags and wore red-white-and-blue visors. A handful of the workers cried as the Model S sedans were lined up on the stage. Tesla was trying to do something big and different, and people were getting hired by the thousands as a result. With machines humming in the background, Musk gave a brief speech and then handed the owners their keys. They drove off the bamboo platform and out the factory doors, while the Tesla employees provided a standing ovation.

Just four weeks earlier, SpaceX had flown cargo to the International Space Station and returned its capsule to Earth—firsts all around for a private company. That accomplishment combined with the launch of the Model S led to a new way in which the world outside of Silicon Valley perceived Musk. The guy who was always promising, promising, promising was doing—and doing spectacular things. "I may have been optimistic with respect to the timing on some of these things, but I didn't overpromise on the outcome," Musk said. "I have done everything I said I was going to do."

After the Model S launch, Musk took his boys to Maui to meet up with Kimbal and other relatives, marking his first real vacation in a number of years. This restful period did not last long, and soon enough Tesla's battle for survival resumed. The company could produce only about ten sedans per week at the outset, and had thousands of back orders that it needed to fulfill. Many investors had started to place bets that Tesla would fail. The critics expected numerous Model S flaws to crop up and undermine the enthusiasm for the car. There were also huge doubts that Tesla could increase production and do so profitably. In October 2012, presidential hopeful Mitt Romney dubbed Tesla "a loser" during a debate with Barack Obama.

With so many people expecting Tesla to stumble and perhaps even go out of business, Musk's bluster mode engaged. He began talking about Tesla's goals to become the most profitable major automobile maker in the world, with better margins than BMW. Then, in September 2012, he unveiled something that shocked both Tesla critics and proponents alike. Tesla had secretly been building the first leg of a network of charging stations. The company disclosed the location of six stations in California, Nevada, and Arizona and promised that hundreds more would be on the way. Tesla intended to build a global charging network that would let Model S owners making long drives pull off the highway and recharge very quickly. And they would be able to do so for free. In fact, Musk insisted that Tesla owners would soon be able to travel across the United States without spending a penny on fuel.

The Supercharging stations, as Tesla called them,

represented a huge investment for the strapped company. An argument could easily be made that spending money on this sort of thing at such a precarious moment in Tesla's history was crazy. Surely Musk did not have the gall to try to revamp the very idea of the automobile and build an energy network at the same time with a budget equivalent to what Ford and ExxonMobil spend on their annual holiday parties. But that was the exact plan. Musk, Straubel, and others inside Tesla had mapped out this all-or-nothing play long ago, and built certain features into the Model S with the Superchargers in mind.

In the latter stages of 2012, Tesla had a lot of Model S reservations. People paid $5,000 for the right to buy a Model S and get in line to purchase. But the company had struggled to turn these reservations into actual sales. The reasons behind this problem remain unclear. It may have been that the complaints about the car's interior and the early kinks mentioned on the Tesla forums and message boards were causing concerns. Tesla also lacked financing options to soften the blow of buying a $100,000 car, and there was uncertainty surrounding the resale market for the Model S. You might end up with the car of the future or you might spend six figures on a dud with no way to sell it.

Tesla's service centers at the time were also terrible. The early cars were unreliable and customers were being sent in droves to centers unprepared to handle the repair volume. Many prospective Tesla owners likely wanted to hang out on the sidelines for a bit longer to make sure that the company did not go under. As Musk put it, "The word of mouth on the car sucked."

By the middle of February 2013, Tesla had fallen into a crisis state. If it could not change its reservations to purchases quickly, its factory would sit idle, costing the company vast amounts of money. And if anyone caught wind of the factory slowdown, Tesla's shares would likely plummet and prospective owners would become even more cautious. The severity of this problem had been hidden from Musk, but once he learned about it, he acted in his signature all-or-nothing fashion.

Musk pulled people from recruiting, the design studio, engineering, finance, and wherever else he could find them and ordered them to get on the phone, call people with reservations, and close deals. Musk told the employees, "I don't care what job you were doing. Your new job is delivering cars." Musk placed Jerome Guillen, a former Daimler executive, in charge of fixing the service issues. Musk fired senior leaders whom he deemed subpar performers and promoted a flood of junior people who had been doing above-average work. He also made an announcement personally guaranteeing the resale price of the Model S.

Customers would be able to resell their cars for the average going rate of similar luxury sedans with Musk putting his billions behind this pledge. And then Musk tried to orchestrate the ultimate fail-safe for Tesla just in case his maneuvers did not work.

During the first week of March, Musk reached out to his friend Larry Page at Google. According to people familiar with their discussion, Musk voiced his concerns about Tesla's ability to survive the next few weeks. Not only were customers failing to convert their reservations to orders at the rate Musk had hoped, but existing customers had also started to defer their orders as they heard about upcoming features and new color choices. The situation got so bad that Tesla had to shut down its factory. Publicly, Tesla said it needed to conduct maintenance on the factory, which was technically true, although the company would have soldiered on had the orders been closing as expected. Musk explained all of this to Page and then shook hands on a deal for Google to acquire Tesla.

While Musk did not want to sell, the deal seemed like the only possible course of action for Tesla's future. Musk's biggest fear about an acquisition was that the new owner would not see Tesla's goals through to their conclusion. He wanted to make sure that the company would end up producing a mass-market electric vehicle. Musk proposed terms under which he would remain in control of Tesla for eight years or until it started pumping out a cheaper, mass-market car. Musk also asked for access to $5 billion in capital for factory expansions. Some of Google's lawyers were put off by these demands, but Musk and Page continued to talk about the deal. Given Tesla's value at the time, it was thought that Google would need to pay about $6 billion for the company.

As Musk, Page, and Google's lawyers debated the details of an acquisition, a miracle happened. The five hundred or so people whom Musk had turned into car salesmen quickly sold a huge volume of cars. Tesla, which had only had a couple weeks of cash left in the bank, moved enough cars in the span of about fourteen days to end up with a blowout first fiscal quarter. Tesla stunned Wall Street on May 8, 2013, by posting its first-ever profit as a public company—$11 million—on $562 million in sales. It delivered 4,900 Model S sedans during the period. This announcement sent Tesla's shares soaring from about $30 a share to $130 a share in July. Just a couple of weeks after revealing the first-quarter results, Tesla paid off its $465 million loan from the government early and with interest. The solid performance of the stock increased consumers' confidence. With cars selling and Tesla's value rising, the deal with Google was no longer necessary, and Tesla had become too expensive to buy. The talks with Google ended.

What transpired next was the Summer of Musk. Musk told his public relations staff that he wanted to try and have one Tesla announcement per week. The company never quite lived up to that pace, but it did issue statement after statement. Musk held a series of press conferences that addressed financing for the Model S, the construction of more charging stations, and the opening of more retail stores. During one announcement, Musk noted that Tesla's charging stations were solar-powered and had batteries on-site to store extra juice. "I was joking that even if there's some zombie apocalypse, you'll still be able to travel throughout the country using the Tesla Supercharger system," Musk said.

Tesla held another press event in October 2014 that cemented Musk's place as the new titan of the auto industry. Musk unveiled a supercharged version of the Model S with two motors—one in the front and one in the back. It could go zero to sixty in 3.2 seconds. Musk also unveiled new software for the Model S that gave it autopilot functions. The car had radar to detect objects and warn of possible collisions and could guide itself via GPS. "Later, you will be able to summon the car," Musk said. "It will come to wherever you are. There's also something else I would like to do.

Many of our engineers will be hearing this in real time. I would like the charge connector to plug itself into the car, sort of like an articulating snake. I think we will probably do something like that."

Thousands of people waited in line for hours to see Musk demonstrate this technology. Musk cracked jokes during the presentation and played off the crowd's enthusiasm. The man who had been awkward in front of the media during the PayPal years had developed a unique, slick stagecraft. Rival car companies would kill to receive such interest and had basically been left dumbfounded as Tesla snuck up on them and delivered more than they had ever imagined possible.

What Musk had done that the rival automakers missed was turn Tesla into a lifestyle. It did not just sell someone a car. It sold them an image, a feeling they were tapping into the future, a relationship. Apple did the same thing with the iPod and iPhone. Even those who were not religious about their affiliation to Apple were sucked into its universe once they bought the hardware and downloaded software like iTunes.

This sort of relationship is hard to pull off if you don't control as much of the lifestyle as possible. PC makers that farmed their software out to Microsoft, their chips to Intel, and their design to Asia could never make machines as beautiful and as complete as Apple's. They also could not respond in time as Apple took this expertise to new areas and hooked people on its applications.

For owners of the Model S and its follow-up, the Model X (an SUV released in late 2015), the all-electric lifestyle translates into a less hassled existence. Instead of going to the gas station, you just plug the car in at night. The car will start charging right away or the owner can tap into the Model S's software and schedule charging to take place late at night, when the cheapest electricity rates are available. Tesla owners also get to skip out on visits to mechanics. A traditional vehicle needs oil and transmission fluid changes to deal with all the friction and wear and tear produced by its thousands of moving parts. The simpler electric car design eliminates this type of maintenance. Tesla still recommends that owners bring in the Model S once a year for a checkup, but that's mostly to give the vehicle a once-over and make sure that none of the components seem to be wearing down prematurely.

Tesla's model shows how electric cars represent a new way to think of automobiles. All car companies will soon follow Tesla's lead and offer some form of over-the-air updates to their vehicles. The scope of their updates will be limited, however. "You just can't do an over-the-air spark plug change or replacement of the timing belt," said Javidan. "With a gas car, you have to get under the hood at some point, and that forces you back to the dealership anyway."

Tesla also has the edge of having designed so many of the key components for its cars in-house, including the software running throughout the vehicle. "If Daimler wants to change the way a gauge looks, it has to contact a supplier half a world away and then wait for a series of approvals," Javidan said. "It would take them a year to change the way the *P* on the instrument panel looks. At Tesla, if Elon decides he wants a picture of a bunny rabbit on every gauge for Easter, he can have that done in a couple of hours."

As Tesla turned into a star of modern American industry, its closest rivals were obliterated. Fisker Automotive, a onetime electric car hotshot, filed for bankruptcy and was bought by a Chinese auto parts company in 2014. Better Place was another start-up that enjoyed more hype than Fisker and Tesla put together and raised close to $1 billion to build electric cars and battery-swapping stations. The company never produced much of anything and declared bankruptcy in 2013.

Tesla easily could have been a member of this defeated bunch, and that's what most people had been expecting. "It is frequently forgotten in hindsight that people thought this was the [worst] business opportunity on the planet," Straubel said. What separated Tesla from the competition was a complete commitment to execute to Musk's lofty standards and an undying belief in Tesla's engineering teams.

17

THE GRAND VISION OF ELON MUSK

THE RIVE BROTHERS USED TO be like a technology gang. In the late 1990s, they would jump on skateboards and zip around the streets of Santa Cruz, knocking on the doors of businesses and asking if they needed any help managing their computing systems. The young men, who had all grown up in South Africa with their cousin Elon Musk, soon decided there must be an easier way to sell their technology smarts than going door-to-door. They wrote some software that allowed them to take control of their clients' systems from afar and to automate many of the standard tasks that companies required, such as installing updates for applications. The software became the basis of a new company called Everdream.

By 2004, Lyndon and his brothers, Peter and Russ, wanted a new challenge—something that not only made them money but, as Lyndon put it, "something that made us feel good every single day." Near the end of the summer that year, Lyndon rented an RV and set out with Musk for the Black Rock Desert in Nevada for Burning Man—a gathering of tens of thousands of people celebrating self-expression and creativity. Lyndon and Musk used to go on adventures all the time when they were kids and looked forward to the long drive as a way to catch up and brainstorm about their businesses. Musk knew that Lyndon and his brothers were angling for something big. While driving, Musk turned to Lyndon and suggested that he look into the solar energy market. Musk had studied it a bit and thought there were some opportunities that others had missed. "He said it was a good place to get into," Lyndon recalled.

After arriving at Burning Man, Musk, a regular at the event, and his family went through their standard routines. They set up camp and prepped their art car for a drive. This year, they had cut the roof off a small car, elevated the steering wheel, shifted it to the right so that it was placed near the middle of the vehicle, and replaced the seats with a couch. Musk took a lot of pleasure in driving the funky creation.

Musk put on a display of strength and determination at the event as well. There was a wooden pole perhaps thirty feet high with a dancing platform at the top. Dozens of people tried and failed to climb it, and then Musk gave it a go. "His technique was very awkward, and he should not have succeeded," said Lyndon. "But he hugged it and just inched up and inched up until he reached the top."

Musk and the Rives left Burning Man excited. The Rives decided to become experts on the solar industry and find an opportunity in the market. They spent two years studying solar technology and the dynamics of the business, reading research reports, interviewing people, and attending conferences along the way. During a session at one of these conferences, representatives from a handful of the world's largest solar installers were sitting onstage, and the moderator asked what they were doing to make solar panels more affordable for consumers. "They all gave the same answer," Lyndon said. "They said, 'We're waiting for the cost of the panels to drop.' None of them were taking ownership of the problem."

At the time, it was not easy for consumers to get solar panels on their houses. You had to acquire the panels and find someone else to install them. The consumer paid up front and had to make an educated guess as to whether or not his or her house even got enough sunshine to make the ordeal worthwhile. On top of all this, people were reluctant to buy panels, knowing that the next year's models would be more efficient.

The Rives decided to make buying into solar much simpler and formed a venture called SolarCity in 2006. Unlike many other solar players, they would not manufacture their own solar panels. Instead they would buy them and then do just about everything else in-house. They built software for analyzing a customer's current energy bill and the position of their house and the amount of sunlight it typically received to determine if solar made sense for the property. They built up their own teams to install the solar panels. And they created a financing system in which the customer did not need to pay anything up front for the panels. The consumer leased the panels over a number of years at a fixed monthly rate. Consumers got a lower bill overall, and they were no longer subject to the constantly rising rates of typical utilities. At the end of the lease, the homeowner could also upgrade to new, better panels. Musk had helped his cousins come up with this structure and became the company's chairman and its largest shareholder, owning about a third of SolarCity.

Six years after that trip to Burning Man, SolarCity had become the largest installer of solar panels in the country. The company had lived up to its initial goals and made installing the panels relatively painless. Rivals were rushing to imitate its business model. In 2012, SolarCity went public and its shares soared higher in the months that followed. By 2014, SolarCity was valued at close to $7 billion.

SolarCity, like the rest of Musk's ventures, did not represent a business opportunity so much as it represented a worldview. Musk had decided long ago that solar just made sense. Enough solar energy hits the Earth's surface in about an hour to equal a year's worth of worldwide energy consumption from all sources put together. Improvements in the efficiency of solar panels have been happening at a steady clip. If solar is destined to be mankind's preferred energy source in the future, then this future ought to be brought about as quickly as possible.

Starting in 2014, SolarCity began to make the full extent of its ambitions more obvious. First, the company began selling energy storage systems. These units were built through a partnership with Tesla Motors. Battery packs were manufactured at the Tesla factory and stacked inside refrigerator-size metal cases. Businesses and consumers could purchase these storage systems to work alongside their solar panels. Once they were charged up, the battery units could be used to help large customers get through the night or during unexpected outages.

Then, in June 2014, SolarCity acquired a solar cell maker called Silevo for $200 million. This deal marked a huge shift in strategy. SolarCity would no longer buy its solar panels. It would make them at a factory in New York State. Buying, rather than manufacturing, solar panels had been one of SolarCity's great advantages. A ton of Chinese, American, and European companies had rushed into the solar panel market and flooded it with equipment. Because there were so many solar panels available for sale, the companies making them were forced to cut the prices of their products to remain competitive with their rivals. This meant that SolarCity could buy panels very cheaply.

For the first few years of its existence, SolarCity had been able to buy these cheap parts while also avoiding the massive costs tied to building and running factories. With 110,000 customers, however, SolarCity had started to consume so many solar panels that it needed to ensure a consistent supply and price. "We are currently installing more solar than most of the companies are manufacturing," said Peter Rive, the cofounder and chief technology officer at SolarCity. "If we do the manufacturing ourselves and take advantage of some different technology, our costs will be lower—and this business has always been about lowering the costs."

SolarCity is a key part of what can be thought of as the grand vision of Elon Musk or the philosophy that links his ideas and companies together. Each one of his businesses is interconnected in the short term and the long term. Tesla makes battery packs that SolarCity can then sell to customers. SolarCity supplies Tesla's charging stations with solar panels, helping Tesla provide free recharging to its drivers. Newly minted Model S owners regularly opt to begin living the Musk lifestyle and outfit their homes with solar panels. Tesla and SpaceX exchange knowledge around materials, manufacturing techniques, and the details of operating factories that build so much stuff from the ground up.

The bonds between the companies extend to the political and competitive spheres as well. It used to be possible for legislators and older companies to gang up on Musk's companies. As of 2012, however, the collective muscle of Musk Co. made such bullying more difficult, as it became harder to go at SolarCity, Tesla, or SpaceX as individual companies. The politicians in states like Alabama looking to protect some factory jobs for Lockheed, or in New Jersey trying to help out the traditional automobile dealerships, now have to contend with a guy who has an employment and manufacturing empire spread across the entire United States. As of this writing, SpaceX had a rocket factory in Los Angeles, a satellite facility in Washington, a rocket test facility in central Texas, and had started construction on a spaceport in South Texas. Tesla had its car factory in Silicon Valley, the design center in Los Angeles, and a giant battery factory in Nevada. SolarCity has created thousands of clean-tech jobs, and it will create manufacturing jobs at the solar panel factory that's being built in Buffalo, New York. Altogether, Musk Co. employed close to thirty thousand people at the end of 2015. The plan is to add tens of thousands more jobs as Musk's companies develop more ambitious products.

One such product arrived in 2015 when Tesla unveiled the Model X. This vehicle used the same foundation as the Model S but shipped as a larger SUV instead of a sedan. The most stunning feature of the Model X was its passenger doors that rose up like wings above the car when opened. The Model X also offered families room for seven people, state-of-the-art safety features, and ways to lug along cargo like skis and bicycles. The major downside accompanying the Model X was its price: the SUV came in even more expensive than the Model S.

Tesla's next car was the Model X SUV with its signature falcon-wing doors. Photograph courtesy of Tesla Motors

At the opposite end of the price spectrum, or so Musk hopes, will be Tesla's third-generation car, or the Model 3. Due out in 2017, this four-door car would come in around $35,000 and be the real measure of Tesla's impact on the world. The company hopes to sell hundreds of thousands of the Model 3 and make electric cars truly mainstream. "I think Tesla is going to make a lot of cars," Musk said. "If we continue on the current growth rate, I think Tesla will be one of the most valuable companies in the world."

Tesla already consumes a huge portion of the world's lithium ion battery supply and will need far more batteries to produce the Model 3. This is why, in 2014, Musk announced plans to build what he called the Gigafactory, or the world's largest lithium ion manufacturing facility. Each Gigafactory will employ about 6,500 people and help Tesla meet a variety of goals. It should first allow Tesla to keep up with the battery demand created by its cars and the storage units sold by SolarCity. Tesla also expects to be able to lower the costs of its batteries while improving them. According to Straubel, the battery packs coming out of the Gigafactory should be dramatically cheaper and better than the ones built today. This would allow Tesla not only to hit the $35,000 price target for the Model 3 but also to pave the way for electric vehicles with five-hundred-plus miles of range.

If Tesla actually can deliver an affordable car with five hundred miles of range, it will have built what many people in the auto industry insisted for years was impossible. To do that while also constructing a worldwide network of free charging stations, revamping the way cars are sold, and revolutionizing automotive technology would be an exceptional feat in the history of capitalism.

For Musk, though, that would not be enough. In August 2013, he unveiled something called the Hyperloop and billed it as a new mode of transportation. You can think of the Hyperloop as a giant tube that sits upon pylons. A pod—filled either with people or supplies—would start at one end of the tube and then be shot toward its destination at about seven hundred mph. The pod would be able to travel so fast because it would be floating on a bed of air, reducing friction. The whole thing would, of course, be solar-powered and aimed at linking cities less than a thousand miles apart. "It makes sense for things like LA to San Francisco, New York to DC, New York to Boston," Musk said at the time. "Over one thousand miles, the tube cost starts to become prohibitive, and you don't want tubes every which way. You don't want to live in Tube Land."

Musk speaks about the cars, solar panels, and Hyperloops with such passion that it's easy to forget they are more or less sideline projects. He believes in the technologies to the extent that he thinks they're the right things to pursue for the betterment of mankind. They've also brought him fame and fortune. Musk's ultimate goal, though, remains turning humans into an interplanetary species. Musk has decided that man's survival depends on setting up another colony on another planet and that he should dedicate his life to making this happen.

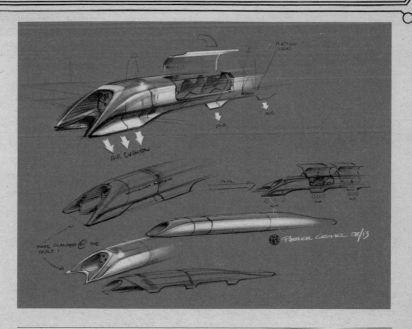

Musk unveiled the Hyperloop in 2013. He proposed it as a new mode of transportation, and multiple groups have now set to work on building it. Photograph courtesy of SpaceX

In the near term, SpaceX will begin testing its ability to take people into space. It wants to perform a manned test flight by 2017 and to fly astronauts to the International Space Station for NASA soon thereafter. The company has also moved into building and selling satellites. Along with these efforts, SpaceX has been testing the Falcon Heavy—its giant rocket capable of flying the biggest payloads in the world—and its reusable-rocket technology. SpaceX landed a rocket for the first time in December of 2015 and has since repeated the feat on a handful of occasions. The company has pledged to let customers reuse these rocket bodies, which would save tens of millions of dollars per flight and totally change the economics of space travel.

In South Texas, SpaceX continues to build out its very own spaceport. It has acquired dozens of acres where it plans to construct a modern rocket launch facility unlike anything the world has seen. Musk wants to automate a great deal of the launch process so that the rockets can be refueled, stood up, and fired on their own with computers handling the safety procedures. SpaceX wants to fly rockets several times a month for its business. Getting to Mars will require an even more impressive set of skills and technology.

"We need to figure out how to launch multiple times a day," Musk said. "The thing that's important in the long run is establishing a self-sustaining base on Mars. In order for that to work—in order to have a self-sustaining city on Mars—there would need to be millions of tons of equipment and probably millions of people. So how many launches is that? Well, if you send up one hundred people at a time, which is a lot to go on such a long journey, you'd need to do ten thousand flights to get to a million people. So ten thousand flights over what period of time? Given that you can only really depart for Mars once every two years, that means you would need like forty or fifty years.

"And then I think for each flight that departs to Mars you want to sort of launch the spacecraft into orbit and then have it be in a parking orbit and refuel its tanks with propellant. Essentially, the spacecraft would use a bunch of its propellant to get to orbit, but then you send up a tanker spacecraft to fill up the propellant tanks of the spacecraft so that it can depart for Mars at high speed and can do so and get there in three months instead of six months and with a large payload. I don't have a detailed plan for Mars, but I know of something at least that would work, which is sort of this all-methane system with a big booster, a spacecraft, and a tanker potentially. I think SpaceX will have developed a booster and spaceship in the 2025 time frame capable of taking large quantities of people and cargo to Mars.

"The thing that's important is to reach an economic threshold around the cost per person for a trip to Mars. If it costs one billion dollars per person, there will be no Mars colony. At around one million dollars or five hundred thousand dollars per person, I think it's highly likely that there will be a self-sustaining Martian colony. There will be enough people interested who will sell their stuff on Earth and move. It's not about tourism. It's like people coming to America back in the New World days. You move, get a job there, and make things work. If you solve the transport problem, it's not that hard to make a pressurized transparent greenhouse to live in. But if you can't get there in the first place, it doesn't matter.

"Eventually, you'd need to heat Mars up if you want it to be an Earthlike planet, and I don't have a plan for that. That would take a long time in the best of circumstances. It would probably take, I don't know, somewhere between a century and a millennium. There's zero chance of it being terra formed and Earthlike in my lifetime. Not zero, but point-zero-zero-one percent chance, and you would have to take real drastic measures with Mars."

Musk spent months pacing around his home in Los Angeles late at night thinking about these plans for Mars and bouncing them off Riley. "I mean, there aren't that many people you can talk to about this sort of thing," Musk said. These chats included Musk daydreaming aloud about becoming the first man to set foot on the Red Planet.

"He definitely wants to be the first man on Mars," Riley said. "I have begged him not to be." Perhaps Musk enjoys teasing his wife or maybe he's playing, but he denied this ambition during one of our late-night chats. "I would only be on the first trip to Mars if I was confident that SpaceX would be fine if I die," he said. "I'd like to go, but I don't have to go. The point is not about me visiting Mars but about enabling large numbers of people to go to the planet."

For employees like Gwynne Shotwell and JB Straubel, working with Musk means helping develop these sorts of wonderful technologies without any recognition. They're the steady hands that will forever be expected to stay in the shadows. If you're Shotwell and truly believe in the cause of sending people to Mars, then that becomes more important than your own desire for glory.

Straubel, likewise, has been the constant at Tesla—a go-between whom other employees could rely on to carry messages to Musk, and the guy who knows everything about the cars. "Elon is incredibly difficult to work for, but it's mostly because he's so passionate," Straubel said. "Some people will get shell-shocked and catatonic. It seems like people can get afraid of him and paralyzed in a weird way. I try to help everyone to understand what his goals and visions are, and then I have a bunch of my own goals too, and make sure we're in synch. Then I try and go back and make sure the company is aligned. Ultimately, Elon is the boss. He has driven this thing with his blood, sweat, and tears. He has risked more than anyone else. I respect the hell out of what he has done. It just could not work without Elon."

Typical employees tend to describe Musk in more mixed ways. They revere his drive and respect how demanding he can be. They also think he can be hard to the point of mean and come off as unreasonable. The employees want to be close to Musk, but they also fear that every interaction with him is an opportunity to be fired. "Elon's worst trait by far, in my opinion, is a complete lack of loyalty or human connection," said one former employee. "Many of us worked tirelessly for him for years and were tossed to the curb like a piece of litter without a second thought."

The prime example of Musk's seemingly callous interoffice style occurred in early 2014 when he fired Mary Beth Brown, his longtime aide. To describe her as a loyal executive assistant would be completely inadequate. Brown often felt like an extension of Musk—the one being who crossed over into all of his worlds. For more than a decade, she gave up her life for Musk, traipsing back and forth between Los Angeles and Silicon Valley every week, while working late into the night and on weekends. Brown went to Musk and asked that she be compensated on par with SpaceX's top executives, since she was handling so much of Musk's scheduling across two companies, doing public relations work, and often making business decisions. Musk replied that Brown should take a couple of weeks off, and he would take on her duties and gauge how hard they were. When Brown returned, Musk let her know that he didn't need her anymore. Brown, still loyal and hurt, didn't want to discuss any of this with me. Musk said that she had become too comfortable speaking on his behalf and that, frankly, she needed a life.

Whatever the case, the situation did not reflect well on Musk. Tony Stark doesn't fire Pepper Potts. He adores her and takes care of her for life. She's the only person he can really trust—the one who has been there through everything. That Musk was willing to let Brown go and in such an unceremonious fashion struck people inside SpaceX and Tesla as the ultimate confirmation of the hard side of his character.

The tale of Brown's departure became part of the story of Musk's lack of empathy. It got bundled up into the tales of Musk humiliating employees in legendary fashion with vicious insult after vicious insult. People also linked this type of behavior to Musk's other quirky traits. He's been known to obsess over typos in emails to the point that he could not see past the errors and read the actual content of the messages. Even in social settings, Musk might get up from the dinner table without a word of explanation to head outside and look at the stars, simply because he's not willing to suffer small talk. After adding up this behavior, dozens of people expressed to me their conclusion that Musk sits somewhere on the autism spectrum and that he has trouble considering other people's emotions and caring about their well-being.

Musk's behavior seems to match up much more closely with someone who is described by neuropsychologists as profoundly gifted. These are people who in childhood exhibit exceptional intellectual depth and max out IQ tests. It's not uncommon for these children to look out into the world and find flaws—glitches in the system—and construct logical paths in their minds to fix them. For Musk, the call to ensure that mankind is a multiplanetary species partly stems from a life richly influenced by science fiction and technology. Equally it's a calling that dates back to his childhood. In some form, this has forever been his quest.

Musk sees mankind as in danger and wants to fix the situation. The people who suggest bad ideas during meetings or make mistakes at work are getting in the way of Musk fixing the problem. The perceived lack of emotion is a symptom of Musk sometimes feeling like he's the only one who really grasps the urgency of his mission. He's less sensitive and less tolerant than other people because the stakes are so high. Employees need to help to the absolute best of their ability or they need to get out of the way.

Musk has been pretty up front about these tendencies. He's begged people to understand that he's not chasing momentary opportunities in the business world. He's trying to solve problems that have been consuming him for decades. During our conversations, Musk went back to this very point over and over again, making sure to emphasize just how long he's thought about electric cars and space.

The same patterns are visible in his actions as well. When Musk announced in 2014 that Tesla would open-source all of its patents so anyone could use the innovations without paying for them, analysts tried to decide whether this was a publicity stunt or if it hid an ulterior motive. But the decision was a straightforward one for Musk. He wants people to make and buy electric cars. Man's future, as he sees it, depends on this. If open-sourcing Tesla's patents means other companies can build electric cars more easily, then that is good for mankind, and the ideas should be free.

One of Musk's most ardent admirers is also one of his best friends: Larry Page, the cofounder and CEO of Google. "If you think about Silicon Valley or corporate leaders in general, they're not usually lacking in money," Page said. "If you have all this money, which presumably you're going to give away and couldn't even spend it all if you wanted to, why then are you devoting your time to a company that's not really doing anything good? That's why I find Elon to be an inspiring example. He said, 'Well, what should I really do in this world? Solve cars, global warming, and make humans multiplanetary.' I mean those are pretty compelling goals, and now he has businesses to do that." As Page puts it, "Good ideas are always crazy until they're not."

The next decade of Musk Co. should be quite something. Musk may become one of the greatest businessmen and innovators of all time. By 2025 Tesla could very well have a lineup of five or six cars and be the dominant force in a booming electric car market. At its current growth rate, SolarCity will have had time to emerge as a massive utility company and the leader in a solar market that had finally lived up to its promise. SpaceX? Well, it's perhaps the most intriguing. According to Musk's calculations, SpaceX should be conducting weekly flights to space, carrying humans and cargo, and have put most of its competitors out of business. Its rockets should be capable of doing a couple of laps around the moon and then landing with pinpoint accuracy back at the spaceport in Texas. And the preparation for the first few dozen trips to Mars should be well under way.

If all of this were taking place, Musk, then in his mid-fifties, likely would be the richest man in the world and among its most powerful. He would be the majority shareholder in two public companies, and history would be preparing to smile broadly on what he had accomplished. During a time in which countries and other businesses were paralyzed by indecision and inaction, Musk would have launched the most successful charge against global warming, while also providing people with an escape plan—just in case. He would have brought a substantial amount of crucial manufacturing back to the United States, while also providing an example for other entrepreneurs hoping to harness a new age of wonderful machines. Musk may well have gone so far as to give people hope and to have renewed their faith in what technology can do for mankind.

This future, of course, remains uncertain. Huge technological issues confront all three of Musk's companies. He's bet on the inventiveness of man and the ability of solar, battery, and aerospace technology to follow predicted price and performance improvement curves. Even if these bets hit as he hopes, Tesla could face a weird, unexpected recall. SpaceX could have a rocket carrying humans blow up—an incident that could very well end the company on the spot. Dramatic risks accompany just about everything Musk does.

This tendency for risk has little to do with Musk being insane, as he had once wondered aloud. No, Musk just seems to possess a level of passionate belief that is so intense and exceptional as to be off-putting to some. As we shared some chips and guacamole, I asked Musk directly just how much he was willing to put on the line. His response? Everything that other people hold dear. He would eventually be willing to give up his family and companies to spend his last years on Mars. "I would like to die on Mars," he said. "Just not on impact."

EPILOGUE

IT WAS NOT THAT LONG ago that the United States had fallen
woefully behind other countries like Russia and China
when it came to launching rockets and putting things in
space. The Space Shuttle—once the workhorse of NASA—
had been retired. American companies like Boeing and
Lockheed Martin could still send up rockets, but they were
too expensive and limited to military use. It seemed that
the United States, which had once dominated aerospace,
would lose this industry entirely—a depressing state of
affairs for a country that prides itself on its inventiveness
and spirit of exploration.

In the middle of 2015, it seemed like SpaceX might
be the next chapter in this sad tale. One of the company's

rockets blew up that June. Doubts surrounded the company over the next few months, as it struggled to identify and fix the problems with the rocket. But then, in December of 2015, SpaceX returned to space in serious style. One of its rockets launched, delivered its payload of satellites, and then returned to Earth, landing with precision. It was the first time a rocket company had pulled off such a feat on a flight for a paying customer.

At almost the same time, Blue Origin, the rocket company of Amazon.com founder Jeff Bezos, landed a rocket too, during a test flight. It later fired off the same rocket, demonstrating that reusable rockets could work. The United States suddenly had the two most exciting rocket companies on the planet. They were accomplishing historic feats and bringing about a future in which cheap flights to space could happen all the time. The rest of the world took notice and has been scrambling to respond ever since.

It seems that we're now living in an age when wealthy technology moguls and bright, energetic engineers are tackling projects that in the past only governments tried to pull off. The rockets, self-driving cars, virtual reality, and artificial intelligence software with almost magical properties are among the inventions that could lead to an amazing century ahead. And, without question, it's Elon Musk who has served as the inspirational guide for this new era. He's the person who appears determined to dream bigger than anyone else.

With its rockets flying well again, SpaceX has turned to manned missions to space and hopes to soon begin taking astronauts—decked out in awesome spacesuits—to the International Space Station and other habitats. For its part, Tesla, in March of 2016, unveiled the Model 3 car. Starting at just $35,000, this is meant to be the all-electric vehicle for the masses. It will bring the latest in automotive software and technology down to an affordable price. About 400,000 people paid to reserve their spot in the waiting line for the Model 3, which turned it into an automotive industry phenomenon. Tesla's autopilot technology has dazzled consumers as well, with its cars already taking over much of the driving duties on highways from humans, with the promise of even more advanced technology coming in the near future. It took Elon Musk almost fifteen years to accomplish his goal of making electric cars mainstream, but the wait seems worth it.

These accomplishments make even Musk's crazier ideas seem possible. When he first announced the Hyperloop in 2013, many, many, many people laughed. Today, there are two start-ups based in California building prototypes of the high-speed transportation system. Hundreds of college and high school students have helped shape the future of the technology too through design contests sponsored by SpaceX. There are plenty of people who genuinely believe we'll shortly see a version of the Hyperloop up and running.

Musk has also set to work building the "space internet." He wants to surround the Earth with thousands of small satellites that will beam the internet down to people from the heavens. This would be a huge deal to the three billion people on the planet who currently cannot access high-speed internet connections either because they're in remote areas or because it's not affordable. It would also give the Earth a backup internet system and pave the way for pushing the internet through space . . . and eventually to Mars. SpaceX has opened an office and manufacturing center in Seattle to build these small satellites, and the workers there may one day modernize the world's communications infrastructure.

The things that Musk chases after are so fanciful that it's easy at times to see him as that Tony Stark type of a figure—more of a fictional being than a human like the rest of us. It's important to remember, though, that Musk's projects do come with a very real human cost. His employees are pushed to their limits and must often trade time with their families and children to stay at the office and try to meet Musk's lofty standards and goals. Musk too has given up on living anything resembling a normal life. His personal relationships have suffered as a result of his ridiculous work schedule. So too has his health. People wanting to emulate Musk may want to be careful with what they wish for.

But there can be little question that Musk does represent something profound, particularly for this moment in the world's history. So many people talk about the problems facing the planet and its citizens. They spend years arguing over ideas, while taking precious little action to try and actually solve the issues. Musk is the antidote to such behavior. He's a man of action.

To that end, Musk trumps Tony Stark and all of his fanciful inventions. He's a real human being who has suffered tremendous personal loss, made great sacrifices, and worked incredibly hard in a relentless quest to pursue his dreams. You may not want to live a life as extreme as Musk's and to give up so much. Musk, though, is a role model for life in the twenty-first century. He's taken on big ideas, found ways to bend technology to his will, and tried his absolute best to ensure that mankind has a bright future.

I, for one, can't wait to see what he does next.

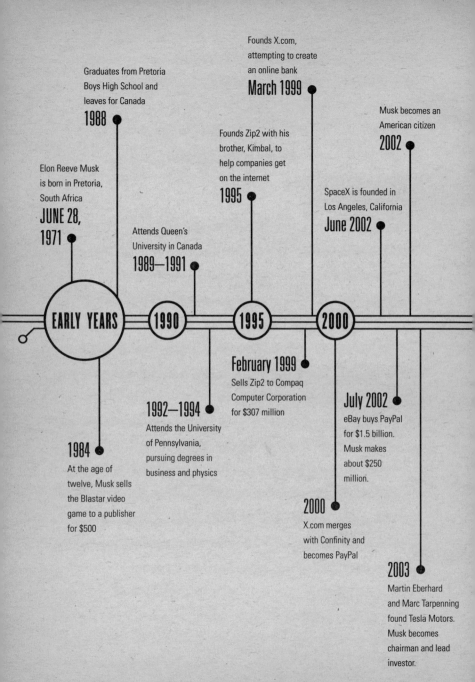

Founds X.com, attempting to create an online bank
March 1999

Graduates from Pretoria Boys High School and leaves for Canada
1988

Musk becomes an American citizen
2002

Elon Reeve Musk is born in Pretoria, South Africa
JUNE 28, 1971

Founds Zip2 with his brother, Kimbal, to help companies get on the internet
1995

SpaceX is founded in Los Angeles, California
June 2002

Attends Queen's University in Canada
1989—1991

EARLY YEARS **1990** **1995** **2000**

February 1999
Sells Zip2 to Compaq Computer Corporation for $307 million

July 2002
eBay buys PayPal for $1.5 billion. Musk makes about $250 million.

1992—1994
Attends the University of Pennsylvania, pursuing degrees in business and physics

1984
At the age of twelve, Musk sells the Blastar video game to a publisher for $500

2000
X.com merges with Confinity and becomes PayPal

2003
Martin Eberhard and Marc Tarpenning found Tesla Motors. Musk becomes chairman and lead investor.

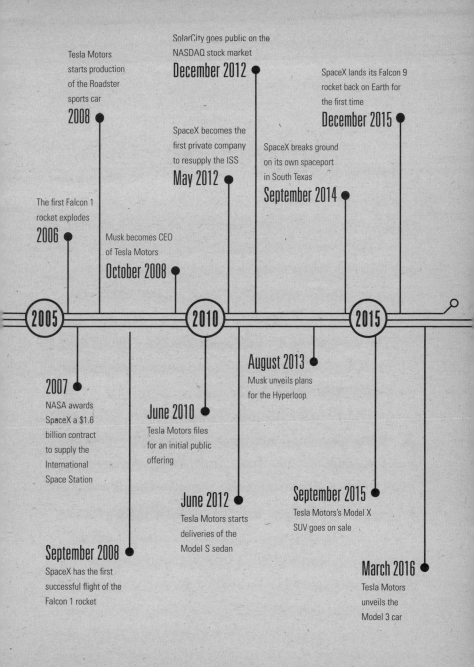

Tesla Motors starts production of the Roadster sports car
2008

SolarCity goes public on the NASDAQ stock market
December 2012

SpaceX lands its Falcon 9 rocket back on Earth for the first time
December 2015

SpaceX becomes the first private company to resupply the ISS
May 2012

SpaceX breaks ground on its own spaceport in South Texas
September 2014

The first Falcon 1 rocket explodes
2006

Musk becomes CEO of Tesla Motors
October 2008

2005

2010

2015

August 2013
Musk unveils plans for the Hyperloop

2007
NASA awards SpaceX a $1.6 billion contract to supply the International Space Station

June 2010
Tesla Motors files for an initial public offering

September 2015
Tesla Motors's Model X SUV goes on sale

June 2012
Tesla Motors starts deliveries of the Model S sedan

September 2008
SpaceX has the first successful flight of the Falcon 1 rocket

March 2016
Tesla Motors unveils the Model 3 car

ACKNOWLEDGMENTS

I'll be forever grateful to the hundreds of people who were willing to give freely of their time, and especially to those who let me come back again and again with questions. There are too many of these people to list, but gracious souls—like Jeremy Hollman, Kevin Brogan, Dave Lyons, Ali Javidan, Michael Colonno, and Dolly Singh—each provided invaluable insights and abundant technical help. Heartfelt thanks go as well to Martin Eberhard and Marc Tarpenning, both of whom added crucial, rich parts to the Tesla story.

Special thanks then to George Zachary and Shervin Pishevar, and especially to Bill Lee, Antonio Gracias, and Steve Jurvetson, who really went out of their way for Musk and for me. And I obviously owe a tremendous debt of gratitude to Justine Musk, Maye Musk, Kimbal Musk, Peter Rive, Lyndon Rive, Russ Rive, and Scott Haldeman for their time and for letting me hear some of the family stories. Talulah Riley was kind enough to let me interview her as well. She helped build a much deeper understanding of Elon. This meant a lot to me, and, I think, it will to the readers as well.

Thanks also to JB Straubel, Franz von Holzhausen, Diarmuid O'Connell, Tom Mueller, and Gwynne Shotwell, who are all among the most intelligent and compelling figures I've run into during years of reporting. I'm forever grateful for their patience explaining bits of company history and technological basics to me and for their candor. Thanks, as well, to Emily Shanklin, Hannah Post, Alexis Georgeson, Liz Jarvis-Shean, and John Taylor, for dealing with my constant requests and pestering, and for setting up so many interviews at Musk's companies. Mary Beth Brown, Christina Ra, and Shanna Hendriks were no longer part of Musk Land near the end of my reporting but were all amazing in helping me learn about Musk, Tesla, and SpaceX.

My biggest debt of gratitude, of course, goes to Musk. When we first started doing the interviews, I would spend the hours leading up to our chats full of nerves. I never knew how long Musk would keep participating in the project. There was real pressure to get my most crucial questions answered up front and to be to the point in my initial interviewing. As Musk stuck around, though, the conversations went longer, were more fluid, and became more enlightening. They were the things I most looked forward to every month. Whether Musk will change the course of human history in a massive way remains to be seen, but it was certainly a thrilling privilege to get to pick the brain of someone who is reaching so high. While reticent at first, once Musk committed to the project, he committed fully, and I'm thankful and honored that things turned out that way.

On a professional front, I'd like to thank my editors and coworkers over the years—China Martens, James Niccolai, John Lettice, Vindu Goel, and Suzanne Spector—each of whom taught me different lessons about the craft of writing. Special thanks go to Andrew Orlowski, Tim O'Brien, Damon Darlin, Jim Aley, and Drew Cullen, who have had the most impact on how I think about writing and reporting, and are among the best mentors anyone could hope for. I must also offer up infinite thanks to Brad Wieners and Josh Tyrangiel, my bosses at *Bloomberg Businessweek*, for giving me the freedom to pursue this project. I doubt there are two people doing more to support quality journalism.

A special brand of thanks goes to Brad Stone, my colleague at the *New York Times* and then at *Businessweek*. Brad helped me shape the idea for this book, coaxed me through dark times, and was an unrivaled sounding board. Thanks, as well, to Keith Lee and Sheila Abichandani Sandfort. They are two of the brightest, kindest, most genuine people I know, and their feedback on the early text was invaluable.

My agent, David Patterson, and editor, Nancy Inteli, were instrumental in helping pull this project off. David always seemed to say the right thing at low moments to pick up my spirits. Nancy did a remarkable job guiding me through the art of turning a complex adult book into something that will hopefully be enjoyable, inspirational, and educational for a younger audience. Thanks so much to you both.

Last, I have to thank my family. This book turned into a living, breathing creature that made life difficult on my family for more than two years. I didn't get to see my young boys as much as I would have liked during that time, but when I did, they were there with energizing smiles and hugs. I'm thankful that they both seem to have picked up an interest in rockets and cars as a result of this project. As for my wife, Melinda, well, she was a saint. From a practical perspective, this book could not have happened without her support. Melinda was my best reader and ultimate confidante. I'm blessed to have such a partner, and I will forever remember what Melinda did for our family.